Taste & See

Other Books by Ginny Kubitz Moyer

Random MOMents of Grace

Daily Inspiration for Women

Taste & See

Experiencing the Goodness of God with OUR FIVE SENSES

Ginny Kubitz Moyer

LOYOLA PRESS.
A JESUIT MINISTRY
Chicago

LOYOLAPRESS.
A JESUIT MINISTRY

3441 N. Ashland Avenue
Chicago, Illinois 60657
(800) 621-1008
www.loyolapress.com

An early version of chapter 16, "The Rosary" appeared on BustedHalo.com on August 13, 2010 as the article "Beads on Call."

Scripture quotations are from the New Revised Standard Version Bible: Catholic Edition, copyright © 1989, 1993 National Council of the Churches of Christ in the United States of America. Used by permission. All rights reserved.

Cover art credit: © iStock/Qweek, © iStock/appleuzr, © iStock/Panptys, © iStock/kowalska-art

ISBN-13: 978-0-8294-4413-1
ISBN-10: 0-8294-4413-0
Library of Congress Control Number: 2016931448

Printed in the United States of America.

16 17 18 19 20 21 22 Versa 10 9 8 7 6 5 4 3 2 1

For Scott,

for everything

And God saw that it was good.

—Genesis 1:10

Contents

Introduction

One fall afternoon about twenty years ago, I was sitting in a college literature course when my professor suddenly made a surprising comment. He referred to Catholicism as a "sensual religion."

Lapsed Catholic that I was, those words grabbed my attention. Sensual? Really? When I thought of my childhood religion, words like *archaic* and *guilt-inducing* were the first to come to mind. *Sensual* didn't even make the short list.

Catholicism aside, to me the words *sensual* and *religion* hardly seemed to belong in the same breath. Wasn't religion something you did with the brain and not with the senses? Wasn't faith all about forsaking that weak, temptation-prone body in favor of the pure and noble soul?

But now, two decades later, I can say that my professor was on to something. In fact, "sensual religion" makes perfect sense to me now. My professor probably had no idea he was imparting a theology lesson, but his one casual comment was the catalyst for me to think more deeply about how I experience faith.

And all that thinking has led me to this realization: if I want to deepen my relationship with God, I need to pay more attention to the senses, not less.

How does God speak to you? If you're like most of us, it's not through a mystical experience or a shimmering vision or a bolt of lightning. When I sit down for evening prayer and think about where I encountered God during the day, my list usually ends up looking a lot like this:

- God was in the mysteriously beautiful lifting of the fog over the hills on the morning commute.
- God was in the conversation with my mom, when she said those encouraging words I needed to hear.
- God was in the spontaneous kiss I got from my son, his little body standing on tiptoe to reach my cheek.
- God was in the taste of fresh homegrown tomatoes, an unexpected gift from a neighbor.

- God was in the sound of the kids playing soccer on the front lawn.
- God was in the smell of the wood smoke that greeted me as I got out of the car from my late-night visit to the grocery store, a smell that made me think of warmth and family.

In other words, God speaks to me not in mystical, abstract ways but through the stuff of daily life. And like any expert communicator, God speaks to me using the language I know best—the language of the five senses.

When I'm participating in the sacraments and rituals of my Catholic faith, the language of the senses is apparent there, too. This *is* a sensual religion, with its art and architecture, its liturgies, its music and chants, its smells and bells. Catholicism proves that something we touch, like a rosary, can prime the mind for prayer. It proves that something we smell, like incense, can lift our thoughts to heaven. Something we see, like a crucifix, reminds us that God became flesh.

That last fact is an essential one to remember if we want to be comfortable with our physical selves. It's sometimes easy to forget that God took on a human body and moved through this world in company with other human bodies—seeing, hearing, smelling, touching, and tasting, and showing that the human body could be a worthy vehicle for the divine. God became flesh, like ours, in the person of Jesus Christ. We miss out on so much if we gloss over that fact, if we ignore the senses in favor of the spiritual without seeing how the two work together.

St. Ignatius of Loyola, the founder of the Jesuit order, certainly understood the connection between the physical and the spiritual. He believed that we can find God in all things—a conviction that lies at the core of Ignatian spirituality. Does God really speak to us through a blue sky, through the sound of laughter, through the taste of dinner? Absolutely, St. Ignatius would say. You don't turn your back on the created world to find meaning and purpose; rather, God reveals himself to us through the very concrete stuff of our lives, through our bodies, through the things we experience with our senses. Walter Burghardt, a twentieth-century Jesuit priest, echoes this idea in these beautiful words:

> To be alive is to look. But not merely with my mind—I am not naked intellect. If I am really to respond to the real, my whole being must be alive, vibrating to every throb of the real. Not only mind but eyes; not only eyes but smell and taste, hearing and touching. For reality is not reducible to some far-off, abstract, intangible God-in-the-sky. Reality is pulsing people; reality is fire and water; reality is a rainbow after a summer storm, a gentle

doe streaking through a forest; reality is a foaming mug of Michelob, Beethoven's Mass in D, a child lapping a chocolate ice cream cone; reality is a striding woman with wind-blown hair; reality is Christ Jesus. (*Tell the Next Generation: Homilies and Near Homilies* [Paulist Press, 1980], 111–12)

Faith is about living life, in all its messy splendor, and doing so with the awareness that God is present throughout it all. It's about recognizing that God speaks to us through our senses and that we can live a richer, more joyful faith if we train ourselves to listen.

This book is a guide to finding God in and through our sensory experiences, from the mundane to the sublime. It's divided into five sections, each one focused on a sense. Within each sense section are five chapters, each highlighting a different experience of that sense. These are experiences drawn from my life and from the lives of others. You'll find some reflections on Bible passages as well.

Following each chapter are prayer steps that invite you to reflect upon the sensory experiences of your own life. They may ask you to ponder the experiences of the day that has just passed or to think more broadly over your life as a whole. All of them are there to help you identify the presence of God in and through the things you see, hear, smell, touch, and taste. These prayer steps are loosely based upon the Examen, the daily prayer that Ignatius taught and that has been a cornerstone of Jesuit spirituality for centuries. (I'll say more about the Examen later.)

As you'll see, many of the chapters deal with common, everyday experiences: hearing the voice of a loved one, admiring the colors of a rose garden, feeling the touch of water on the skin. Some of them deal with specifically Catholic topics, such as praying the rosary or going to confession. If these chapters feel particularly personal, it's because my own faith story is there; the sensual nature of Catholicism was the very thing that drew me back into the church in my mid-twenties, and is in large part responsible for keeping me there ever since. So if you were once Catholic but feel distant from the faith, these chapters and prayer exercises can help you see an old religious tradition from a new perspective. If you are a practicing Catholic, these exercises might help you attend more mindfully to the presence of God in what you already do, both inside and outside of church.

Wherever you are on your journey and whatever that journey happens to be, I hope this book helps you discover what St. Ignatius knew: you truly can find God in all things. All it takes is a willingness to pray with your senses and an openness to the idea that God craves a personal connection with you. And if "sensual religion" still feels like an oxymoron to you, as it did to me at first, let yourself trust that the senses are not a barrier to faith. You will find that they are five powerful entry points for God's goodness to become known to us—and God seizes that opportunity every day of our lives.

How to Use This Book

For as long as people have prayed, they have prayerfully reflected upon their daily experiences. It was during the sixteenth century that St. Ignatius of Loyola came up with the particular formula that we know today as the daily examen. In his book *The Spiritual Exercises*, he describes the five steps, paraphrased here:

1. Give thanks to God for his many gifts.
2. Ask for grace to honestly acknowledge your mistakes and sins.
3. Review your day, looking at your feelings, words, actions.
4. Identify any shortcomings in how you lived your day.

5. Look ahead and resolve, with God's grace, to do better.

For centuries, countless Christians have found this a useful ongoing daily prayer. I find that it opens my eyes to the small movements in my spiritual life and helps me recognize God's presence in even the seemingly mundane parts of my routine.

Over the years, many people have introduced variations on the basic structure of the examen. For example, in his helpful book *A Simple, Life-Changing Prayer: Discovering the Power of St. Ignatius of Loyola's Examen*, Jim Manney explains that he reverses the order of Steps 1 and 2, finding that it is easier to be grateful for God's gifts after first asking for God's grace. I'm fond of this change for exactly the reason that Manney gives: invoking God's grace before I even start praying helps remind me that God is an equal partner in this prayer and that it's not just about my own memory or perspective.

In this book, I've taken the basic elements of the examen—ask for grace, give thanks, review the day, make a resolve for the future—and used that as the inspiration for the prayers following each chapter. Like other authors, I've made a few changes. For example, I've combined Steps 3 and 4 into one section, simply called Review, because the idea of examining our personal shortcomings is not applicable to most of the topics presented here. Likewise, you'll find that some prompts ask you to look back over the past twenty-four hours, while others invite you to think about your life experiences more broadly.

How quickly should you go through the book? One approach is to read one chapter and its corresponding prayer each day. Another way is to take a space of more than one day between chapters to explore these practices, which can be a beneficial way of helping the ideas and insights sink in for a time.

Is there a particular time of day to do these prayers? Many people pray the examen in the evening, finding it a helpful spiritual wind-down from the day and a good way to plan ahead for the next day. As a mom, I know from experience that evening prayer often turns into unintentional snooze-time, so this may not work for you. Early morning, a lunch break, or late afternoon may be better. Go with whatever works and whatever keeps you coming back.

Each examen in this book has multiple questions. While I've tried to make these reflection prompts as universal as possible, some may feel more relevant than others to your age or stage in life. If a question doesn't resonate with your situation in life, or if it just doesn't speak to you, feel free to skip on to one that does. That said, if you find yourself spending a lot of energy trying to avoid a certain question, then that could be a sign of something deeper there, something worth exploring in prayer. Ignatian spirituality is about being attuned to the stirrings of our souls, so spend time reflecting on any questions that provoke a strong reaction, either negative or positive. It may be the first step in a process that helps you deepen your relationship with God and your understanding of his plan for you.

Ultimately, this is a book for you, and whatever approach you take is the right one. Use it at your own pace and in your own time. I hope it is a rewarding and enjoyable journey through God's gift of the five senses.

Sight

In the Gospel of Mark, the blind beggar Bartimaeus approaches Jesus with a request: "My teacher, let me see again" (Mark 10:51). And Jesus gives him the gift of sight.

It must have been so astonishing for Bartimaeus to experience that sudden shift from darkness to light. What was the first thing he saw? Was it the blue sky, the dusty road stretching before him? Maybe it was an olive tree or the surprised faces of the crowd. But I like to think that the first thing he saw was Jesus, standing mere inches in front of him, the man who opened his eyes to all the rest.

In the story of this blind beggar, we're invited to think about our vision. Do we ever take sight for granted? Are we sometimes so caught up in our problems that we are blind to the wonders of the world around us? This story is a challenge, a nudge to think about our own habits. I know I need that, on some days more than others.

But I love that this story is more than just a challenge. It's also a promise that if we open up our vision, we too will see God in the world around us, closer to us than we realize.

1
Color

One of my favorite moments in the movie *The Wizard of Oz* comes when the house has just landed with a thump in Munchkinland. With no small amount of trepidation, Dorothy makes her way to the front door and slowly, slowly, opens it. As she does, the entire film changes from black and white to vivid Technicolor.

It's an abrupt shift, one that must have been dazzling to 1939 movie audiences who were still unaccustomed to seeing color on the big screen. And no matter how many times I've seen the movie over the years, that scene still makes me catch my breath. In that moment, I'm reminded of something that I usually take for granted: we live in a world that is alive with color of every shade and hue.

When I was a child, it seemed that every color in Munchkinland and on earth could be found in a box of sixty-four Crayola crayons. I always got such joy out of breaking the perforated seal of a new box and tilting back the cardboard lid, revealing rows of sharply pointed, unused crayons—everything from brick red to sea green.

Smaller boxes of crayons were never quite as satisfying. The box of eight had only one shade of blue, whereas the box of sixty-four offered me everything from periwinkle to turquoise. Those crayons were a vocabulary of color, communicating my imaginative visions. I could make my drawing look exactly as I had pictured it in my mind because I had the tools to do so, all lined up like choir members in their cardboard stalls. Even at a young age, I was learning that color is a language and that the more words you have, the richer your experience of living.

Though I wield crayons less often now than I did thirty years ago, I am still just as susceptible to the power of color. And as an adult I've found that it's very gratifying to focus throughout the day on a particular color and to look for all the shades of it I can find. When I take an afternoon to look for orange in the world around me, it seems to pop up everywhere:

the rust of an autumn leaf, the brightness of a traffic cone, a slice of cheddar cheese, a child's T-shirt, the construction paper behind a piece of art mounted on a café wall, the coral of the evening sky. I realize that there is far more orange out there than I ever realized, and that thought cheers me, maybe because it shows that both God and humanity can't be limited to a basic palette of color. There is a visual abundance all around me, and it is very, very good.

It was sometime during the Crayola years that I first read the picture book *People* by the Dutch illustrator and author Peter Spier. It's a meticulously detailed book celebrating the diversity of people and cultures on earth. The cover itself, a white background highlighting a crowd of people of all colors and sizes and in ethnic forms of dress, is a visual celebration of the variety to be found in the human family.

Two illustrations in particular have remained vivid in my mind all these years. On the second-to-last page, we see a cityscape in which all the buildings are the same shade of ochre, all the people have the same skin color, and all the clothing is the same olive gray. It's like looking at a horrible dystopia. The book asks us to think about how dull it would be if we all looked alike.

Then you turn the page, and you have a city street scene blazing with life and color: different skin tones, different colors of clothing, buildings of all styles and shapes, and flags of varying hues. And you realize that life is far more interesting when we all look different from one another.

Living in the diverse San Francisco Bay Area is sort of like living in the last two pages of that picture book. I sit in a café and look around me, and the range of skin tones includes everything from pale white to light olive to rich brown. If you were to draw the people around me, you'd need several different crayons to faithfully represent all these complexions, as if God's creative vision couldn't be limited to just one. Sometimes that page from the Peter Spier book flashes into my consciousness: how boring it would be if we all looked alike. And when we humans are at our finest, the most like the God who made us, we recognize that variety of color as something to celebrate.

People and plants, crayons and cars, flowers and food—every day we live and move in the middle of a kaleidoscope of color. And though I often take it for granted, it's always better when I don't. I'm always happier when I choose to be Dorothy for a day, opening the door of complacency and letting myself be dazzled by the colors right before my eyes.

Begin

Take a few slow breaths. Center yourself and open up to feel God's presence. Ask for God's grace as you enter this time of prayerful reflection.

Give thanks

Think about the variety of colors in the world. Ponder the fact that the human race reflects that diversity. Give thanks to God for treating us to such visual richness.

Review

Go back through your day, and think of the colors that you saw. Take a moment to recall some of the most memorable ones, the ones that caught your eye in particular.

Try looking at your immediate surroundings. How many different colors do you see? Really notice them, and the variety.

Think of times when you have experienced the diversity of humanity. When have you seen that diversity as something to celebrate?

Have you ever wished that everyone else looked more like you? Speak to God about this.

Look ahead

Tomorrow, choose a color. Pay attention to all the variations of that color you encounter over the course of the day. If it helps to keep a written list of the things you see, do so. As you admire the colors, think about them as a testament to God's creative abundance.

2

Gazing

Gaze is a lovely word. Unlike *stare*, which has connotations of impoliteness and intrusiveness, *gaze* implies a certain reverence for the object of one's viewing. It implies taking time to notice, to marvel, to enjoy.

We gaze at sunsets, at museum artwork, at the face of a newborn. We gaze at the things we love. We sometimes lose track of time when we gaze; we seem to know that what we're doing is worthwhile in and of itself. Gazing is not something we rush.

And if you're like me, it's not something you do much of anymore.

Over the past few years, I've realized that my attention increasingly seems to flit from one thing to the next. I guess

I can blame my busy life, with its ragged balance of job/family/commute/writing/cleaning/sporadic exercising. Who has time to look deeply at anything anymore? My mind is often on the next item on my mental to-do list, and my eyes follow.

Also putting a crimp in my ability to gaze is technology. With the Internet there is more to see than ever before. Every Web site has multiple images and links vying for my attention; if one isn't interesting, I can quickly and easily move on to the next. In my purse is a rectangular device that lets me take this habit anywhere I go. Now I don't even have to look at the world around me as I wait in line to order at the café. I can look down at my phone, scrolling from one status update to the next. There is a constant stream of images ready to load, waiting for the touch of my finger; I don't need to linger on any one for any length of time.

It makes me wonder about myself, and about humanity as a whole. Are we losing our ability to look deeply? Are we forgetting what it means to focus on one thing, and only one thing, to let our eyes drink in the sight of someone or something, to get to know that thing so well that we could draw it faithfully, not omitting a single detail?

The Victorian Jesuit poet Gerard Manley Hopkins had the gift of gazing deeply. In his journals, he observes nature with astonishing levels of detail. In one passage he describes the

August sky, and how it looked different when he held up his hand to the light:

> Putting my hand up against the sky whilst we lay on the grass I saw more richness and beauty in the blue than I had known of before, not brilliance but glow and colour. It was not transparent and sapphire-like, but turquoise-like, swarming and blushing round the edge of the hand and in the pieces clipped in by the fingers. (*Poems and Prose of Gerard Manley Hopkins* [Penguin Books, 1953], 109)

There's such precision in his descriptions, as if he had nothing more pressing to do than savor the exact appearance of the world before his eyes. A hand held to the sky doesn't seem to matter much in the scheme of things—but when you look more closely, isn't it really an object of wonder and awe? Do we miss that little miracle when we let our eyes dart restlessly from one thing to another, always looking for some new stimulation?

If we simply let our gaze rest, do we connect with life—and with God's goodness—more deeply?

After the Indian Ocean tsunami of 2004, I heard a news story that haunted me. A reporter was talking about a distraught mother who was trying to locate the infant who had been ripped out of her arms by the floodwaters. This mother gave a detailed description of her baby, hoping desperately that, by some miracle, the child was alive and being cared for by a stranger. In her description of the child, she mentioned the fact that one of his ears was slightly larger than the other. "It is the kind of detail that only a mother would know," said the reporter, and in that comment I felt the full force of the tragedy. This was a mother who had gazed at her baby, who knew this child so well, every tiny detail of him, in the way that mothers do. To know that the object of that loving gaze had been lost, probably forever, made me understand the grief of that tsunami in a way nothing else could.

I never heard the outcome of the story, but as I think of that mother now, wherever she is, I hope the memories of her child sustain her in some way. I hope that the gazing she did before that terrible moment filled her with memories that can't be taken away and that no natural disaster can destroy. She will not see that child grow up, but the time she spent gazing at him was precious, holy time, fixing an image of him and his face and his ears in her heart for as long as she lives.

Gazing also has a role to play in prayer. A few years ago, I read Anthony DeMello's book *Sadhana: A Way to God*. In it, he describes a prayer exercise recommended by St. Teresa of Ávila, one that is deceptively simple: imagine Jesus looking at you, lovingly and humbly. In other words, just sit and let Jesus gaze at you.

The first time I tried it, I imagined Jesus looking straight at me, at close range, with love and humility in his eyes. It felt awkward; my immediate impulse was to look over my shoulder to see who was standing behind me. Then I turned back, and Jesus was still looking at me with infinite love and a smile that seared my heart, and I found myself crying.

I was not prepared for the power of that gaze. Throughout my life I've seen many images of Jesus looking directly at the viewer from a painting or an icon, but they always seem stern and solemn, as if Jesus were reading the hidden sins of humanity as a whole. With this exercise, I was fixed in Jesus' gaze, and it was directed at no one but flawed little me, and Jesus was smiling. I could not escape the love in those eyes, or the fact that it was intended for me. *I'm not worthy*, I kept thinking, but the more I sat there, the more I began to believe that perhaps I am. I started to believe that maybe Jesus is a little easier on me than I am on myself, that he sees my flaws but he also sees beyond them, to the very best of me, the heart of who I really am.

Becoming the object of so loving a gaze is an exercise that never fails to move me. *Don't you get tired of looking at me?* I think. *Don't you want to look at someone shinier and better, someone who has it all together?* And yet the more I stay with it, the more I realize that Jesus is happy just to keep his eyes on me. I sit and let myself be warmed by that gaze, the gaze of a Savior who loves me enough to want to memorize every detail, the Jesus who knows which ear is larger than the other, and how many hairs are on my head, and all the other details too.

It is a form of love, gazing deeply. Maybe it's also a form of love to let down our guard and allow ourselves to be seen.

Begin

Take a few slow breaths. Center yourself and open up to feel God's presence. Ask for God's grace as you enter this time of prayerful reflection.

Give thanks

Reflect on your ability to gaze. Even if you don't do it often enough, thank God for your ability to look at one thing for a long time. Ponder the reality of Jesus, who looks at us with humility and love.

Review

With God, take a walk through your day. What did you really look at today? What captured and held your gaze?

Were there things you did not take time to look at, even though they may have been worthy of your gaze? What distracted you?

Practice gazing right now. Look at one thing in your line of vision. Keep looking. Try to describe it in words for someone who does not see it. What are you noticing?

Look ahead

Try the prayer exercise mentioned above. Find a comfortable, quiet place, and imagine that Jesus is looking at you lovingly and humbly. See him gazing at you. Don't forget to look back into his eyes. Let yourself feel the love in his eyes, a love directed at no one else but you.

3

Created Beauty

Roses are a treat for multiple senses. Their scent is justly famous, and it's hard to think of a flower with smoother, more velvety petals. But when I think of why I love roses, the first thing that comes to mind is their beauty.

This beauty is on vivid display in the municipal rose garden in the city where I live. Large, well-established rosebushes grow in the middle of a park, bordered by brick walkways. When these flowers are blooming, it's like walking around inside an artist's paint box.

I see pale delicate yellows and bright flashy pinks. I find red roses that look like passion on a stem growing next to blooms of cool, elegant lavender. There are petals of tiger-lily orange and others of stark white—so white that it seems to have gray undertones. And there are roses with two colors, like my grandmother's beloved Double Delights, light yellow and raspberry pink, looking almost good enough to eat.

The names are almost as evocative as the colors. In our city garden, each rosebush has a little placard at its base, like a name tag at a party. They read like a gallery of famous people: Henry Fonda, Pope John Paul II, Julia Child, Johann Strauss. Some of the names suggest action and activity: Blastoff or Strike It Rich. Other roses are named for virtues, such as Lasting Love, Honor, or Sweetness. Perhaps the award for best name goes to the rose in the front of my own house, an orange with gradations of red and yellow, a rose that echoes any color you put next to it. It's called Perfect Moment, and I can't think of a better way to describe what it's like to be in a rose's company.

They make me so happy, these beauties. I often think of a quotation from the nineteenth-century minister Theodore Parker: "Every rose is an autograph from the hand of the Almighty God." Roses are visible proof that God is real, and that it's possible for us mere mortals to get very, very close to the Divine.

The fascinating thing about roses, though, is that they're not just the work of God. They are a visual testament to the work of humans as well.

The roses in the rose garden—and the ones in my own yard—are not wildflowers. They are the result of hybridization, the process of cross-breeding rose plants to create a new variety. Developing roses is a science and an art, one that requires knowledge and experience and patience. Many of the roses I love to look at did not even exist a century ago. The Mr. Lincoln rose in my front yard, with the deep red petals, was born in 1964. The yellow and pink Peace rose, a perennial favorite, was not introduced to the U.S. until 1945.

I suppose that this knowledge could diminish my enjoyment of the rose garden, but it doesn't. If anything, it enhances it. I look at them, and I think about how the municipal rose garden, with all its blazing variety of color, is a collaborative work between God and us. It's true that many beautiful things on this earth—the ocean, the sky, the mountains—are God's work, not ours. But other beautiful things—like a carefully planned flower bed, a symmetrical avenue of trees, a garden of rocks and succulents, a hybridized rose—come from human minds and hands.

All of this bears witness to the fact that, as humans, we don't want merely to admire natural beauty; we also want to be actively involved in creating it. Making one small patch of the planet nice to look at is like doing, in miniature, what

God did in creating the oceans and land. Maybe that's why gardening feels like an almost-sacred pastime or why most of the gardeners I've met tend to be such spiritual people. Even if all I'm doing is putting a small marigold in a pot for the patio or clearing the flowerbed of weeds, I'm tapping into the artistic nature of the divine, and it feels good to do it.

I have to believe that God appreciates our efforts to enhance the world's appearance, both the grand efforts and the small ones. It must be gratifying for God to see what kind of beauty a gardener or a horticulturist can bring into being. I imagine that God encourages the rose experts in the same way a parent gives a child a box of paint and says, "You don't need to keep the colors separate. Mix them up! I want to see what you can make!" When a master artist encourages a protégée, everyone benefits.

So when I walk around the brick pathways of the city rose garden, I sometimes recall that saying about how roses are autographs from the hand of God. I certainly agree, though when I look out at the stunning variety of colors, I'm tempted to take the metaphor a step further. God writes the autograph, but we help mix the ink. And that's a collaboration worth celebrating.

Begin

Take a few slow breaths. Center yourself and open up to feel God's presence. Ask for God's grace as you enter this time of prayerful reflection.

Give thanks

Reflect on the beauty of the created world. Ponder the people who support and continue God's creative work through gardening, landscaping, conservation, or other activities. Give thanks for the roles they play in enriching your life.

Review

With God, take a walk through your day from start to finish. Where did you see the beauty of the natural world?

Think about how that beauty got there. Was it God's work alone, or were humans involved too?

Was there beauty that you ignored or missed? If so, what distracted you?

When have you helped make the world more beautiful to look at?

Look ahead

Think about tomorrow and ask God to help you open up to the natural beauty around you. Pray for the grace to notice and savor the sky, the trees, the flowers in your neighborhood, the evening light. Choose one way that you can make the world more beautiful to look at—even something as simple as picking up a piece of garbage—and think of the Creator God as you do.

4

Incense

Incense. The very word can make our noses tingle with remembered fragrance. It's a pungent, unmistakable smell, one that scents the air of so many moments in our Catholic lives.

That's why it's ironic that my most powerful experience of incense did not involve my nose but rather my eyes.

This happened during a Sunday morning Mass at St. Dominic's Church in San Francisco. Built in the 1920s, it seems centuries older, a soaring Gothic church that looks like a bit of medieval Paris plunked down in the city by the bay. It was the eleven-thirty Mass, one that my family does not usually attend; it has a full traditional choir and lots of incense and is longer than most Masses, which makes it challenging to attend with kids. But it was a beautiful service, and as it came time for the Gospel to be read, the acolyte came down off the altar, swinging the thurible of incense, walking ahead of the priest as he carried the Gospel to the pulpit.

The priest gave the homily, and as I listened to it, I noticed something in the air. When I say "in the air," I mean it quite literally. The morning sunlight was streaming in through the large stained-glass window to my left. In that huge oblong shaft of light, I saw the incense, hanging there in the sunlight, spreading and moving upward, slowly and gently, like a beautiful shifting veil. It was glorious and arresting all at once, almost like a living thing. The homily, good as it was, couldn't compete with that beautiful mesmerizing haze, which changed moment by moment.

Seeing it, I was suddenly aware of the air in which it was hanging. It looked like air made visible, a potent and beautiful reminder of something I take for granted. Unless I'm having one of my periodic mild bouts of asthma, I don't tend to think of the air around me; I breathe it and otherwise ignore its existence, even though it is one of the very things that makes my existence possible.

But that morning, with the smoke of the incense spreading itself across my line of vision, I was reminded of the presence of air. It took something else—in this case, a ritual of my faith—for that most essential thing to become visible to me.

Life is full of these ordinary miracles, the taken-for-granted things that support our fragile life on this globe. They are not just air and water and sunlight, but also things so close to me that I often ignore their existence: things such as love, the ties of family and friends, the way our bodies work and heal themselves, and the return of spring after the blasts of winter. I live in the middle of these things, yet I don't often *see* them. Like the air, they're too close, too constant, always edged out of my consciousness by the more flashy stimuli that demand my attention. I need something else to point out their existence.

In fact, I realize that my experience with the incense reveals a fundamental truth about the power of faith. It is significant that it took a church ritual for me to notice something I take for granted, that it took the practice of my faith to nudge me into a sense of awe and wonder at what surrounds me always. Throughout my adult life, I've found that Catholicism is central to my happiness because it does exactly this: it helps me see things.

Sometimes this happens through the sacraments, which are, by their very nature, visible signs of God's invisible grace. Sometimes it happens with a homily that speaks to the latest struggle of my life. Sometimes it happens with prayer, which provides a chance to pause and notice and marvel at the way the various disconnected parts of my life actually belong together.

And once, on a bright Sunday morning, it happened with incense, curling up to the rafters and helping me see the very air that makes all the rest of it possible.

Begin

Take a few slow breaths. Center yourself and open up to feel God's presence. Ask for God's grace as you enter this time of prayerful reflection.

Give thanks

Ponder God's love and grace. Give thanks for the invisible things that sustain your life, the things you either can't see or see so often that you tend to forget their existence.

Review

Think about one of your own "incense in the air" experiences, or about a time when faith helped you see something more clearly. Where were you? What did you learn?

What miracles did you see today? Were you aware of them as they were happening?

Consider prayer as the incense that helps you identify moments of God's grace in your life. What kind of prayer can you practice each day that might help you see life's ordinary miracles for what they truly are?

Look ahead

Tomorrow, find a place in which to sit quietly for five minutes. It might be in your home, outside somewhere, or in a church. Close your eyes and pray to God, asking for an awareness of the many little miracles that sustain your life. Then open your eyes, look around you, and identify as many of these miracles as you can.

5

Church Architecture

According to my best calculations, between ages eight and fourteen I attended 406 Masses. This estimate includes both Sunday services with my family and the liturgies I attended at my Catholic school, where the entire student body headed en masse to Mass for First Fridays and holy days of obligation.

If you'd looked at me during any of those Masses, I'd probably have come across as being rather pious. You'd find me sitting quietly in the pew, following all the responses, to all outward appearances a model little churchgoer.

Inside, though, I was often deeply bored. Sure, I liked the music, and I would sometimes enjoy the Gospel readings, but Mass can be a hard sell for a kid. Looking for something to do, I learned to focus my attention on my visual surroundings, committing them to memory.

The church we attended was St. Simon, a large rectangular church built in the 1950s. The stained glass was relatively modern, large chunks of colored glass making up pictures of keys and chalices and other holy-looking things. The altar piece was impressive, featuring a huge mural of the Crucifixion, with saints Simon and Jude looking on solemnly. Lining the perimeter of the church were the Stations of the Cross—highly detailed oil paintings that I always liked to look at. So although the sounds of the Mass were not regularly inspiring, my eyes had plenty to engage them: the statue of Mary and the infant Jesus, the little alcove holding candles and a painting of Our Lady of Guadalupe, the vivid red carpet around the altar.

There was a certain comfort, a centering effect, in being in such a familiar place. Even if I found it boring, church functioned as a sort of You-Are-Here, the red dot on the map. It was a constant in my life, a place I knew by sight, an interior I knew by heart.

Fast-forward to college. Once I flew the family nest, my Mass attendance dropped off dramatically. I attended Mass on Easter, Christmas, and maybe once or twice more, if I were visiting home. While I had logged in approximately 240 Masses in four years of Catholic elementary school, I attended about twenty in four years of college. When I did attend, my thoughts would wander just as they had during my elementary school years, but with a difference: thanks to the quasi-independence and intellectualism of my college experience, my mind had far greater pastures in which to roam. I was questioning the basic morality I had been taught, the historical foundations of Catholicism, even the value of organized religion—why go to Mass if I was feeling so distinctly disconnected from the church? I could hardly see the point. More and more, it seemed to me that a private and personal spirituality was the only way to live, that a big structure like the church could never be anything other than dysfunctional and insular. And though I never stopped calling myself Catholic, I'd hedge by saying that I "was raised Catholic." The passive voice pleased me; this Catholic identity was something my parents chose for me, something firmly seated in my past, reflecting neither my present nor my future.

It was during my junior year in college that a subtle shift occurred. I studied for a semester in Paris, and shortly after my arrival, the program of which I was a part took all the students on an outing to the basilica of Sacré-Coeur, the striking white building perched atop the hill of Montmartre. Construction began in 1875, making it one of the newer churches in town, but to a native Californian it was plenty old enough to be impressive.

It was the first non-American church I had ever entered, and the moment I walked in, it dazzled my eyes. It was darker than the churches I was used to, which created a palpable sense of mystery. All around me were tall white statues surrounded by long thin tapers, lit like Spanish exclamation points. The light flickered in the gloom of the cavernous space, as if it were glowing with prayer and tradition. It was a far cry from the rectangular 1950s-era Silicon Valley church of my childhood; this church had contours and nooks, and I could not get enough of it. I had the sense that I was seeing the history of my childhood religion—that this represented, in some obscure way, the roots of my faith, even though that faith was something I was no longer sure I wanted. *This is where you came from*, the dimly lit place full of statues and candles seemed to say. It captivated me. I could not look away.

During that semester of study, and then a year and a half later when I returned to Paris to teach English, I kept finding myself drawn to churches. I loved visiting them, dropping by on a weekday afternoon to wander and gaze at the stained glass and stone. I got to know some of them well; my favorite was Saint-Sulpice, with its two massive towers, its Delacroix murals, and the candleholders, where centuries' worth of flames had traced black wings on the walls. I even went to Mass a few times, once to Saint-Sulpice on Easter morning and once to Notre-Dame to pray for an end to the month-long Parisian public transit strikes. (If you have ever experienced the French on strike, you know that I was asking for a miracle.)

Though I still wasn't willing to call myself Catholic by choice, being in those churches did give me the sense of being part of something larger than myself. Notre-Dame was older and more visually impressive than my childhood church in California; those soaring ceilings and stained glass and that famous rose window were visual proof that, for centuries, people had been motivated by the search for the sublime. They had felt that there was something beautiful about practicing religion, and they wanted their surroundings to reflect that. Standing where they had stood, I began to understand the link between the eyes and the soul.

Back home, acclimating again to life in California, I missed the history and splendor of those European churches. As a master's student at Stanford, I decided one day to attend

Mass at Memorial Church, the glorious centerpiece of the campus. Though it was less than a hundred years old, it had much the same grandeur and majesty of those Parisian cathedrals, and I wanted to satisfy my thirst. I was going more for the architecture than anything else, I told myself.

Yes, it was beautiful, with its glorious mosaics, its intricate stained glass, its Romanesque contours. Visually, it did not disappoint. But I soon found myself coming back for reasons that had nothing to do with architecture.

Run by two Dominican priests, the Stanford Catholic community was a place where students were both challenged and encouraged. The two priests obviously loved their ministry; so too did the lay choir, the lectors, and the Eucharistic ministers. I expected that my eyes would be satisfied by the beauty of the building, and they were; but I also discovered that my soul was fed by the homilies, which were rich in depth and substance. Those homilies showed that intellectualism was not the enemy of religion, as I had thought in college, but was its complement. I was surprised by how much I could enjoy attending Mass.

After a time, I began to attend after-Mass young-adult dinners and social events. I made friends with my fellow young adult Catholics. I could ask my questions about faith and found that others were asking them too, and that the process was holy in and of itself. I kept coming back to church, always wanting more, and always—without fail—finding it.

Seventeen years later, that is still true. In the Mass, in the practice of my faith, I find something even beyond beautiful architecture. I find the framework that makes all the rest of my life make sense. I no longer say that I was raised Catholic. I say that I am Catholic, and it is a perfectly comfortable statement to make.

Writing all this, I acknowledge that my journey fits a pretty predictable pattern. I'm hardly the first cradle Catholic who practiced her faith as a child and teen, moved away as a college student and young adult, then came back in her mid-twenties. My story is the story of many others, and yet for each of us, it's deeply personal and profound. I don't have any regrets for the years I spent disengaged, because they were necessary ones. I needed them so I could be free to make my own choice about faith, eyes wide open.

When I look back, I realize that my sense of sight played an integral role in my return to the church. It was the beauty of those Parisian churches that got me dipping my big toe, however slightly, in the water of Catholicism again. It was the beauty of the Stanford church that got me to immerse myself fully. It's a potent witness to the power of a lovely worship space; beauty is able to reach beyond the eyes and into the soul, reawakening memories and giving voices to our hungers . . . maybe, even, helping us satisfy them.

And though I still have a fondness for soaring, magnificent cathedrals like the ones in Europe or at Stanford, a church doesn't have to be fancy to satisfy my eyes. I get the same positive feeling when I walk into any church, ancient or modern, extravagant or plain, because when I look around even the most modest church, I recognize the visual signposts of my life as a Catholic: the candles, the altar, the red sanctuary light, the tabernacle. I see those things and I'm at peace, because I know that my journey has brought me home.

Begin

Take a few slow breaths. Center yourself and open up to feel God's presence. Ask for God's grace as you enter this time of prayerful reflection.

Give thanks

Give gratitude to God for the faith communities to which you have belonged, past and present. Reflect on your desire to connect with others in faith. Thank God for the physical places dedicated to worship and for the people who have built them.

Review

Take some time to think of memorable worship spaces you have seen. Were you a tourist, an active participant, a curious guest? What are your strongest visual impressions of those places?

Think of a church or place of worship in which you have spent a lot of time. What did it look like? What visual memories remain foremost in your mind as you recollect it?

How has that particular place helped shape your life of faith?

Are there any worship spaces you've seen that you desire to see again? If so, why?

Look ahead

Visit a church or place of worship when a service/Mass is not going on. Take some time to pray quietly and simply to look at what is around you. Notice what pleases you, what captures and holds your gaze. Say a prayer for the people who worship there regularly, that their faith journeys will be rewarding ones.

Hearing

If I'm honest, I must confess that my ability to hear is frequently responsible for increasing my stress level. My high-school students are excited about Homecoming Week, and I can't redirect their chatter. My kids are playing with a toy robot that makes space-age *piu piu piu* noises as I'm trying to finish a writing project. The neighbor's dog won't stop barking, there's a car alarm that has been going off for five minutes, and the phone is ringing with the tenth solicitation call of the day.

It's enough to make me want to break out the earplugs, retreat to the desert, or both.

On days like this, I need to remind myself of all the ways that sound is good. I need to review all the ways it restores my soul and enhances my life.

I think of music, which calms me and feeds my imagination. There are wise words of advice, coming just when I most need to hear them. The uniqueness of a friend's voice, that audible fingerprint, reminds me of the blessing of her life. Even the annoying noises, considered from a new angle, are evidence of the connections and commitments in my life that I would never choose to give up.

With a small change in perspective, I can recognize sound for what it is: one more powerful way God reveals himself to me, day after day.

6

Voices

It took me by surprise. I was replaying messages on my answering machine, deleting the overfull in-box, when my friend Mary spoke to me for the first time in over a year.

"Hi, guys," she said in her musical voice, which always seemed to cover a wider range of notes than most people's.

I stood there in the bedroom, looking at the answering machine, letting the message play. It was a long one, as Mary's messages tended to be; she had the endearing tendency to ramble, to share every thought as it came to her. This particular message was not, in its substance, especially earthshaking. She had missed a call of ours because she was napping and was offering a mea culpa, hoping to reschedule a time to see us.

But Mary had died of cancer, and this was the first time since her death that I had heard her voice. And for a few brief moments, after a year's worth of grief and loss and the slow climb toward acceptance, she felt very much alive.

We don't gather voices of our loved ones the way we gather pictures. Maybe, with the advent of smartphones and digital recording devices, that is changing; it's certainly easier to record a conversation now than it used to be. But, though most of us have many reminders of what our loved ones look like, we have fewer reminders of the way they sound.

And yet voices are astonishingly unique, each one such an integral part of our experience of another person. We are all fearfully and wonderfully made, as Psalm 139 says, and our voices are one of the most potent aspects of that.

Voices are slippery things to recall, though. When I try to remember the voice of a person I no longer hear, I often flounder. My grandmother, who died when I was sixteen, was a very influential part of my life, but her voice hovers just outside the reaches of my memory. When I try to reconstruct it, the result is vague and unsatisfying; I'm never quite sure I'm getting it right.

Voices also change, even if we aren't aware of it. My boys' voices have evolved over the course of their short lives, growing progressively deeper, a process that will only continue but is easy to overlook in the day-to-day work of raising them. I stumble upon a video of them as toddlers, and as I hear their squeals and high-pitched little-kid voices, I am suddenly reminded of endpoints in their development that have slipped by so gradually that they flew below my radar. There will come a day when they will have deep, masculine, adult voices, and the voices I hear today will belong to a time long past. I want to capture the here and now, to have a backup for my memory, which I know will not be as reliable as I would hope.

So there is something precious about these audio files, on cameras or film or answering machines. Hearing Mary's voice that day made her suddenly real to me, in a way that the photo of her on my prayer table can't do. In that moment, her physical presence seemed nearer to me than it had since her death, as if the triggers of sound also reactivated my memories of how she used to smell and what it felt like to hug her. It was an almost eerie experience in which time barreled backward to something I thought I had forgotten. I was used to remembering her with my eyes; now I could remember her with my ears, too, and the remembering was painful but mostly very, very sweet.

There will come a time when the voices of the people we love, which we hear so often that we sometimes tune them out, are no longer a part of the sounds that make up our days. That's why there is something to be said for recording their voices and for listening mindfully even as they speak of mundane things such as looking for their keys or scheduling an appointment. Because there will come a time when we'd give anything to hear a loved one's voice telling us that he needs to pick up the dry-cleaning or that she will be a bit late for dinner.

And there will come a time when a casual message left on an answering machine is more than just a few seconds of recorded sound. It's the echo of a person who can never be replaced, only remembered.

Begin

Take a few slow breaths. Center yourself and open up to feel God's presence. Ask for God's grace as you enter this time of prayerful reflection.

Give thanks

Take a moment to ponder the people who are important to you. Give thanks to God for them, and for the uniqueness of each one. Take a moment to thank God for the fact that, at every stage in your life, you have encountered people whose presence has enriched your life.

Review

Starting with this morning, review the voices you heard today. Think of the unique sound of each one.

Think of people you love who have died. As much as you can, try to hear each one's voice again. This is often easiest if you think of a phrase or saying your loved one liked to say. If there is a way to listen to a recording of his or her voice, do so.

Think of someone you love who is still alive but whose voice you have not heard in a while, maybe because you tend to communicate electronically, or maybe because you have been too busy to connect in person. Try to recall the last time you heard his or her voice.

Look ahead

Call someone you care about, someone you normally would e-mail or text. Even if the conversation is a short one, pay attention to the sound of his or her voice. If this were the last time you could hear this person speaking, what would you remember?

7

Background Noise

My house is a noisy house. This is the reality of living with two active boys, whose play often involves chasing, wrestling, running, kicking a ball around the house, or sending toy vehicles careening at mad rates of speed over our hardwood floors.

Even before I had kids, though, I often found home too noisy for prayer. When I felt the need to pray deeply, I'd leave and go somewhere else, looking for true silence. Many times I found it at a local church, the one my grandparents used to attend. It's a large high-ceilinged church, with beautiful stained glass and wonderfully retro statues of saints who look as if they came right out of 1950s central casting: St. Thérèse of Lisieux with her sweet smile and red lips and armful of roses, St. Patrick with his shamrocks.

Some afternoons I was the only one there. I'd genuflect, cross myself, slip into a pew somewhere near the back, and pray quietly, letting the peace of the place seep into my bones.

Looking back on those moments now, I marvel at how my prayer life has changed. I rarely go to that church anymore; it's too far outside my triangle of home/work/boys' school, the little orbit of my suburban working-mom existence. Leaving that usual path would make me feel like a satellite going rogue, and I just don't go rogue much anymore.

It's easy to romanticize the stillness of those quiet-church afternoons, to consciously contrast it with the never-ending noise of my life now. Those days, my prayer happened in perfect silence; it was God and me, with no other sounds to distract me.

Or was it?

When I think back to that quiet church, I remember hearing noise there, too. There was the wind outside, rustling the branches of the trees. There was the noise of the building as it settled, a periodic little creaking that would come out of nowhere and go again, a brief but unmistakable wheezing of

the wood. There was the sound of a door opening or closing somewhere behind me in the vestibule, an unseen visitor
doing business that did not take him or her into the main
body of the church.

The sounds were not long or sustained. They did not
invite my participation or demand my immediate attention,
but they were unmistakably present.

Perhaps true silence is not a state that others have achieved
and I haven't. Perhaps it's not as easy to find as I'd thought.

For my last birthday, my husband gave me the gift of a
weekend retreat of my choice. To fully understand what this
meant to me, you should know that my last retreat had
been eight years before, when I was pregnant with my first
child. I've always loved the chance to leave normal life behind
for a weekend, to have the space to unwind and relax into
self-awareness and a closer union with God, so I greeted this
gift with great rejoicing.

After doing a little research, I chose a weekend at the local
Jesuit retreat house, a place I'd been to a few times over the
years. It happened to be a silent retreat; other than the pre-
sentations and the prayers and Masses, no one would speak
during this retreat. I wouldn't be chatting over the dinner

table; I wouldn't be saying hello to the folks I passed in the courtyard.

In other words, it would mean going rogue in a pretty major way.

Though I was excited, the idea also made me somewhat apprehensive. Silence seemed like a foreign concept to me, something I'd long forgotten and which my body had learned (more or less) to do without. Would the introduction of silence be like drinking caffeine after years away? I feared it would be an utter shock to the system, equal in magnitude to taking a desert hermit to the first row of a heavy-metal concert. Could I handle it?

As it turned out, I needn't have worried. It was a weekend without conversation, yes—but that doesn't mean it was silent. Even in the beautiful, remote retreat center hugging the side of a hill, there was noise. In fact, the lack of human voices meant that I heard all the other sounds operating on a sublayer below the clamor of speech: the *drip drip* of the tap in my bathroom; the swish of the legs of my jeans rubbing together as I walked; the rustle of dry leaves on the path that heralded the swift movements of a lizard; the low whine of an airplane; the clang of a door closing; the small swift birds chirping as they hopped around the dew-wet lawn in the morning; the startling, feathery flap of wings as those same birds, busy building a nest in the eaves, swooped off at my approach.

Even the evening prayer in the quiet small chapel, silent and still and magical in the candlelight, was punctuated by sound. The first night I was there, praying quietly with a few other retreatants, I heard the meow of a cat outside. Actually, it was more than a meow; it was almost cartoonish, like a cross between a yowl and a gargle. It sounded like a person pretending to be a cat. It went on and on, and though I looked when I went outside, I couldn't find the cat.

I heard it the next night too, during evening prayer. This time it seemed to move, first on my right side, then on my left. It went on and on, the same odd yowl at the same odd pitch, and I could tell from the muffled laughter of the woman in the pew behind me that I wasn't the only one hearing it.

Was the cat hurt? I know next to nothing about cats, but the sound didn't seem like an everyday feline noise. My prayer was soon edged out by macabre visions of a small kitten trapped under the foundation of the chapel, wasting away, desperately in need of rescue. My desire to follow the rules of silence did temporary battle with my concern for the well-being of the piteous creature yowling night after night. Concern won.

I approached the elderly brother who was hosting the retreat, busily stacking prayer books in the back. "I keep hearing a cat. Is it hurt?" I asked him, in a voice so low he had to cup his hand to his ear. I raised my voice slightly and repeated the question.

"Oh, that cat," he said in loud exasperation. "Don't worry. It's just in heat."

That un-silent silent weekend points to a larger reality. Maybe perfect stillness—the kind you imagine you need in order to have the rich spiritual life of the saints and mystics—is impossible to come by on this earth. I can never entirely rid myself of background noises. And maybe that fact is not something to regret but to embrace.

Because all those noises—the resonant echo of the kneeler in my grandparents' church, the yowl of the cat in heat, the sound of a car driving down the street when the kids are in bed and I am savoring the quiet house—remind me that I'm not alone. They are proof of the forces of nature, of time, of geology, of other people. They are a reminder that I live not in a vacuum of perfect silence but in the middle of a dynamic world. Taking deliberate steps to tune down the noise is good and helpful, but if the noise never completely goes away, perhaps that's not really a problem. If I reach for perfect silence and get frustrated when I don't achieve it, I am setting myself up for frustration.

And really, this noise is a reminder of my mission as a follower of Jesus Christ. My faith doesn't belong in a soundproofed chamber, insulated from the world around me. It is something that is played out in the midst of kids, and amorous cats, and traffic, and doors that slam. It is a faith that, at its best, helps me engage more mindfully and Christfully with others, with people who are heard as well as seen.

Begin

Take a few slow breaths. Center yourself and open up to feel God's presence. Ask for God's grace as you enter this time of prayerful reflection.

Give thanks

Take some time to ponder your ability to hear. At times it seems like a curse, but recognize it for the blessing it is.

Review

In your memory, scroll through the sounds you heard today. (This might be easiest to do if you just focus on one setting or one place where you spent time today.) Which noises pleased you?

Which ones were annoying? Which ones did you try to block out?

Think for a moment about the sources of the annoying noises. Even if you didn't like the noises themselves, see if there is a way to be grateful for the people or things that caused them.

What are you hearing right now as you reflect?

Look ahead

Take some time tomorrow to sit quietly for five minutes—in a park, in a café, in your own home. Let yourself feel God's presence. Pray, and when you hear a background noise, remind yourself that it is not an intrusion but a part of this complex, beautiful world in which you live. Pray a blessing for the source of that noise.

8

Music

As a child, I believed in a future full of promise. Although the specifics of adulthood were vague, one thing that never wavered was my innate conviction that the years to come would hold many wonderful things. *When I grow up I will travel to all those places I love to read about in books. When I grow up I will be anything I want to be.* Over the years, the dream jobs on my list included nurse, veterinarian, ballerina, writer, and—for one extraordinarily brief period—nun.

When I became a teenager, my hopes for the future grew both more varied and more urgent. The desires for travel and a fun livelihood were joined by the longing for true love, as well as the thirst for adventure beyond my suburban existence. Much of teenagerhood felt like biding my time, waiting for exciting and dramatic things. Yet, with the optimism of an adolescent, I had every reason to believe that they'd materialize eventually. The future held great promise; I could feel it.

Now, in my early forties, that sense of unlimited possibility is far less intense than it used to be. I won't say it's totally gone; I believe in a God who wants us to live abundantly and fully, whether we are eight or eighty. But the feeling has become muted over the years, if only because I am increasingly aware that my time on this earth is finite and that much of it has already passed. How can I avoid the nagging, insidious thought that the best is already behind me? How can I recover that childlike certainty that an abundance of beautiful things still waits for me?

Two answers come to mind: prayer and music. And, as I've learned, they often feel very much like the same thing.

My music collection includes several movie soundtracks, but my favorite is the score from the Italian film *Cinema Paradiso*. This movie tells the story of Toto, a small boy in a Sicilian village. Growing up without a father, Toto is taken under the wing of Alfredo, the movie theater projectionist. Toto develops a reverence for films, for the magic of what happens when a group of people gathers in the darkened silence of a movie house. He grows up, falls in love with a local girl, and leaves for the army. Later, he becomes a famous director and returns to the small village upon hearing about the death of Alfredo. A surprise awaits him, and I won't say more for fear of spoiling an ending that seems to touch everyone who sees it.

The score by Ennio Morricone and his son Andrea Morricone is justly famous. There are four main themes in the soundtrack, three of which correspond to the various stages of Toto's life. One represents his childhood, while another—called "Maturity" on the soundtrack—underscores his reflective return home. Arguably the most well-known of the three is the theme that accompanies his first passionate foray into romantic love. I'm about as good at describing music as I am at describing wine, but suffice it to say that this theme ranges across the keyboard. It rises, it falls, and in that way it mimics the ups and downs of love.

My best friend, Amy, and I saw the movie for the first time when we were in high school. We became instant fans. The actor who played the teenage Toto had a lot to do with our enthusiasm, but even his Italian good looks did not blind us to the beauty of the storyline and the music. At that time, cassette tapes were just giving way to compact discs, and the soundtrack was one of the first CDs I bought.

My family fell in love with the music, too. We'd listen to it on car trips down highway 101 to visit my grandmother or to see my sister, who was attending college four hours' drive away. The swell of the romantic theme would fill the car as we drove through brown rolling hills or through California's Central Valley with its long straight rows of vegetables. "This music just propels you along the highway, doesn't it?" my mom remarked at one point. She was right; with the music in the background, the drive felt like flying. And for me, the teenager in the backseat, the music seemed to affirm my innate certainty that someday I, like Toto, would live a life of romance, excitement, and emotion.

The CD came with me to college, where I listened to it often on the boom box in my freshman dorm room. Looking back, I realize that the movie's core themes corresponded beautifully to the transition into college life. The movie was about childhood, which I had left behind in my first move out of the family nest. It was about the glory and the thud of love, which I sensed was in my future. And it was about going back and revisiting the life I once knew, finding that some things are familiar but many are changed. I remember a letter from our family friend Linda during that first year of college; she wrote about seeing *Cinema Paradiso*, which had touched her deeply with its themes of nostalgia and home. "You can never really go back, except in your memory," she wrote. That freshman year, I was starting to discover the truth of that. My visits home were nice but different, because I had changed and a threshold had been passed. Home was still home, but it was now one of a few places I could claim as my own, instead of the only one.

That change made me more happy than wistful, though. My world was finally beginning to expand, just as I had hoped it would. And there was no better soundtrack for this reality than *Cinema Paradiso*, the beautiful score that promised me, implicitly and in a way I could not explain, that good things lay ahead.

I listen to the music now, in my car, ferrying my kids around in the daily predictability of my suburban existence. It's been more than twenty years since I first heard it, but that soundtrack still has the power to touch me deeply. There's a different quality to my listening now, because the music has delivered on its tacit promise; I've known romance, I've known loss, and I've ventured far beyond the boundaries of home. So many of the things I hoped for as an eighteen-year-old have happened, plus more besides.

And I'm no longer the young Toto who looks at life as a limitless blank slate. The backward-glance of the middle-aged Toto, confronting the mortality and fragility of those we love, is what speaks to me most powerfully now. Even writing that, I feel a bit of a jolt. It would have been inconceivable to me, sitting on the floor in front of the VCR at Amy's house, to see the teenaged Toto and immediately think of how young he looks.

And yet even in my fifth decade of life, there's something in those notes that still sings of promise. Listening to the soundtrack is a prayer; it orients me gently toward God, the source of all creation and beauty. It's God who fills us with the desire for a life of meaning, a life in which we venture beyond boundaries and try new things, trusting that our efforts will bear fruit. It's surely the same desire that leads a composer to sit at a piano and experiment, confident that all the tunes have not yet been written and that there still are melodies waiting to be discovered. I hear this well-loved music and find myself believing, with something like my youthful certainty, that the universe is full of wonderful possibilities that I'll never be able to exhaust.

That's what this film score does for me. It's what all great music does, I think. No matter how young or old we are, it keeps propelling us forward, into the promise of the beautiful unknown.

Begin

Take a few slow breaths. Center yourself and open up to feel God's presence. Ask for God's grace as you enter this time of prayerful reflection.

Give thanks

For music. For composers, instrumentalists, singers, those who help record and distribute the music you love. For the people who introduced you to the songs and melodies you love.

Review

Think of the most beautiful songs and musical pieces you know. It might help to write a list.

Choose one. When did you hear it for the first time? What memories or associations does it bring up for you?

Think of a time when music made you feel that something good was waiting for you or lifted you beyond the present. Do you feel that way about life as a general rule, or do you tend to think that "the best is behind"? If so, allow God to challenge that notion.

Look ahead

Seek out a piece of music that has always made you feel hopeful. Listen to it again, letting yourself be open to its implicit promise. Tomorrow, go throughout the day trusting that good things await you.

9

Encouragement

I was turning twenty-seven, and instead of excitement at my approaching birthday, I felt like a student who had failed to live up to her full potential.

For years, I'd had a specific vision of what my adulthood would be like. Get married by twenty-five and have my first child about two years later; that was the future I had plotted out for myself. It didn't matter that this timeline had been conceived when I was about fifteen and therefore far too young to know better. All that mattered was that I had multiple friends who were married, engaged, or in long-term relationships, while I was none of the above. And although I knew I should be above such petty feelings of comparison and jealousy, I wasn't. News of friends' engagements provoked a two-sided, Janus-like reaction for me: on the one hand, honest and unfeigned happiness for them; on the other, the feeling that their personal milestone was like a microscope, magnifying my own incomplete existence in a way that I just could not ignore.

One day shortly before my birthday, I was standing in my friend Suzanne's classroom. We were team-teaching an American studies class. I valued her sense of humor, her command of the history side of the curriculum, and her practical approach to life. We bonded not just through lesson-planning but also through hikes in the foothills and the occasional excursion over the hill to a brewery on the coast, where we and a group of our fellow teachers would sit on a patio, look out over the ocean, and feel the stress of school and life recede behind us.

It would make a better story if the words she said to me had been uttered in that setting, overlooking the blue horizon. In reality, the conversation took place in a portable classroom, about twenty minutes before the first bell rang. Somehow my approaching birthday entered the conversation, and in a moment of frankness I told her I wasn't looking forward to it. "All my friends are getting married, engaged, you name it," I said. "I thought by the age of twenty-seven, I'd be there too."

She looked me right in the eye. "So you aren't married yet? So what?" she said. "Don't compare yourself to other people. You are on no one's timeline but your own."

You are on no one's timeline but your own.

Maybe it doesn't sound like much now, but at the moment—and, in fact, for years afterwards—those words went right to the heart of my need. They nudged me out of the comparison game that we fall into, even with people we love, the one that can erode our relationships if we aren't careful. They helped me see that the focus needed to be on me, myself, not in a selfish way but in a liberating one. Life would unfold for me at the pace it was meant to. That one life, that one pace, was the only one I needed on my radar.

And, subtly, her words made me think that perhaps the timeline I'd constructed for myself was not the one I was meant to live. Perhaps there was some larger pattern to my life, one that did not involve an early marriage and kids before thirty and which would bring me the fullest level of joy and meaning if I respected it for what it was and did not constantly feel the need to make it fit into someone else's framework.

We all have experienced a conversation like this sometime in our lives, some life-altering moment when we hear words that break us free. They may be words of advice when we're feeling stuck between two choices. Maybe they are words of comfort when we feel broken. They may even be the words that give us a hard truth that we have been avoiding, words we don't like to hear in the moment but which we later recognize as being the catalyst for a change that sets us free.

In the Gospels, we come across the power of words often. Jesus challenges the Pharisees with strong words. (They seem never to listen to his advice—but if they had?) He also offers parables and wisdom to instruct the crowds. In the Gospel of Luke, when a woman in the crowd calls out, "Blessed is the womb that bore you and the breasts that nursed you," Jesus responds with, "Blessed rather are those who hear the word of God and obey it" (Luke 11:27–28). I used to dislike this passage, which seemed a little too dismissive of Mary, but now I see it differently. It's a promise that holiness is not available to the privileged few but to all of us.

I wonder how these words were received by that unnamed woman in the crowd. Had she been unfavorably comparing herself to the blessed mother of this astonishing man? When Jesus spoke those words, did she suddenly realize that holiness was within her own grasp too? It's possible that other people heard these words from Jesus' lips and were also changed, suddenly realizing that a life of meaning was not something you fell into but something you created for yourself by your actions. Maybe this entire exchange touched the soul of more than one hearer, helping them—like me—learn that the comparison game is a game with no winners.

I have learned over the years that when we hear such words coming from the lips of others, we're hearing the Holy Spirit speak through them. I have never yet heard a booming divine voice in my ear, St. Paul-style. God has (thus far, I guess) not chosen to communicate with me that way. But when I pray the examen and review my day and think about the conversations I've had, I realize how much God speaks to me through the voices of my children, my husband, my friends, my students, my neighbors, my colleagues. It may very well be that I have been God's voice for other people too, without even knowing it.

I hope I have, because I know the power of being on the receiving end of that kind of wisdom. And I know what a relief it is to hear the voice that calls us out of the place where we're stuck and directs us to the truth that we can't find on our own.

Begin

Take a few slow breaths. Center yourself and open up to feel God's presence. Ask for God's grace as you enter this time of prayerful reflection.

Give thanks

Reflect on wisdom, wherever it shows up. Give thanks that we are able to find perspectives other than our own. Offer gratitude for the people in your life who care about your well-being.

Review

Think of people in your life you would consider wise. Remember a specific time when one of them said something that stuck in your mind.

How did those words shape you? What changed in your life as a result of hearing that advice?

Have you continued to let those words guide you, or have you fallen back into your old way of thinking?

When have you been a voice of encouragement to someone else?

Look ahead

Take a moment to hear wise words of advice again as if for the first time. Write them on a piece of paper or put them somewhere you will see them tomorrow. Let those words guide you as you go throughout your day.

10

Confession

Guilt knows no religious boundaries; if you're human, you've surely felt it. That said, I think there's a reason for all those jokes about the tenacity of Catholic guilt. For many of us, this faith can become a fertile field for the weeds of regret to grow and flourish in. And they're often tough to pull out, those little suckers. The roots go deep and cling.

Over the years, I've learned a few important things about guilt. The first is that not everything that makes you feel guilty is actually a sin. It has taken me a long time to realize that. But I've also learned that when you do honestly have something for which you need forgiveness, there is a sacrament for that. And, for most of us, it's a sacrament in which

God's healing love comes to us not through our eyes or nose or mouth but through our ears.

Like many cradle Catholics, I can't talk about guilt without talking about confession, and to talk about confession, I have to scroll back to second grade. That was the year of first Reconciliation, our inaugural experience of this sacrament that is all about naming one's sins and wiping the slate clean.

Of course, when it came to shedding guilt, the ritual of confession wasn't the only option. Our teachers told us that we could speak directly to God in prayer and ask for forgiveness. But with the sacrament of confession, we would actually hear another human being say, "Your sins are forgiven; go in peace." The priest would stand in the place of Jesus Christ, and we'd leave with the words of absolution in our ears and, thus, in our hearts.

When the evening of our first Confession arrived, our families escorted us to church, where the two parish priests were waiting. Rather than have us recite our sins in the darkness of a confessional, the teachers felt that a face-to-face meeting with the priest would be less intimidating, so I met with our pastor, who was sitting in an armchair, smiling encouragingly. As maiden voyages go, it was pretty smooth sailing.

That was the first of many confession experiences, most of which took place during the school day. A few times a year, up until we all graduated in eighth grade, our teachers would take the class as a whole over to church for confession.

No matter what grade we were in, these visits followed a particular format. First, we took some time in the classroom to individually review our sins, called an examination of conscience. Often the teacher led the examination, reading aloud a list of possible sins ("Have I taken the Lord's name in vain? Do I fight with my brothers and sisters?"). Then we filed over to the church, a horde of awkward, silent, blue-plaid penitents.

The more I went to confession, the less I liked it. It was unnerving to kneel down in the pitch-black confessional, waiting in suspense for the screen to slide back, indicating that Father was ready. The darkness was intense, just a line of light under the door. And there was something undeniably spooky about speaking to a disembodied voice coming from a person visible only as a shadowy outline on a linen screen.

But my biggest problem was that I rarely had anything significant to confess.

Sure, there were times when I had a specific transgression or two on my conscience; I was hardly a perfect kid. But I was pretty good, and more often than not, I'd struggle to come up with confessable sins. I was respectful of my parents. I didn't hit my sister or even fight with her all that much. As for coveting a neighbor's wife—whatever that meant, I was pretty sure I hadn't done it. But I couldn't decline confession on the grounds of being too good; there had to be *something* on my conscience.

So I got creative. In fact, preparing for confession became less a spiritual exercise than an intellectual one; I became an expert in taking neutral actions from my past and reframing them as transgressions. In the darkness of the confessional, I shared all kinds of pseudo-sins: "Bless me, Father, for I have sinned. My mom asked me to set the table, and I dawdled ten minutes before doing it." I used that one often over the years.

It gave me something to say, but it came with a price. I ended up becoming so good at this creative interpretation of guilt that, as I grew up, my conscience became finely tuned to anything in my life that could be construed as wrong. As I moved into adolescence, guilt became a frequent companion: I felt bad about not being friendly enough to someone I'd met or about not doing my homework as thoroughly as I could have.

To be fair, I can't place the blame for this entirely on my confessional experiences. No doubt psychological hardwiring and genetics had something to do with this. In fact, one might say that perhaps I was more sensitive to the guilt messages of my Catholic past *because* of my innate tendency toward anxiety. But whichever came first, there's no question that there was a powerful symbiosis between the two. Certainly, the message that I couldn't be anything other than sinful helped to feed my emerging anxieties.

During my teenage years, obsessive-compulsive disorder began to make its first entrance into my life, and the guilt problem grew significantly worse. Without warning, random upsetting thoughts sometimes flashed into my mind, as if it were asking, *What is the worst thing I could be thinking right now?* If I saw a knife on the kitchen counter, I thought, *What if I pick that up and stab someone?* If I was holding a baby, I thought, *What if I dropped this baby?* I was so suffused with guilt for having had such thoughts in the first place that I couldn't move past them. *Only a bad person would get stuck thinking such thoughts*, I'd tell myself. Even when I finally confided in my parents and learned to classify my struggles as OCD, my finely tuned sense of guilt would not relinquish its hold on me. And guilt is a great fertilizer for OCD. In the classic vicious-cycle scenario, my fears and anxieties multiplied as I moved through my high school career.

It was around this time that my visits to confession stopped. My high school didn't have scheduled confessions as my previous school had done. Although I had certain warm memories of the feeling of lightness and closure that came from being forgiven for a legitimate sin, my dominant memory of confession was sitting there in the classroom desk, casting about frantically for something I could present as a sin. There was not much incentive to go, so I didn't.

It was in college that I formally and vocally went on a confession strike. As my self-awareness grew, I began to consciously connect the dots of my emotional life, and for the first time I saw the link between some of the sin-based instruction I'd received as a child and the chronic guilt I suffered from. And I became angry. "There is absolutely nothing healthy," I told friends, "about taking a kid and insisting that she is sinful and training her to feel guilty. In fact," I said, roused to anger, "confession does nothing but cultivate neuroses and damaging emotions."

I didn't blame my former teachers for this; they had known nothing about my private struggles to come up with confessable sins. Nor did I blame my parents, who had always communicated a very balanced sense of right and wrong.

Rather, I blamed Catholicism in general for what I saw as its dour insistence on the pervasiveness of sin. On the rare occasions I would go to Mass, certain lines would leap out at me: "O Lord, I am not worthy to receive you," was one. *Enough with the unworthiness*, I'd think angrily. *My problem is that I need to feel MORE worthy.*

With my increasing distance from Catholicism, with my resentment toward a church that put so much emphasis on sin and guilt, I was sure I'd never willingly go back to confession again. *When I commit a legitimate sin,* I told myself, *I'll go directly to God and ask for forgiveness. I don't need the dark box, the floating voice.* I resolved never to darken the door of a confessional again.

Years passed as I finished college and went to Paris, then on to graduate school. Thanks to the terrific priests at Stanford and the community of thoughtful young adults there, I was seeing a different face of Catholicism, one that allowed for questions, for debate. Over the next three years, the walls between me and the church began to erode steadily; there was light coming through for the first time in a long while. But even as I returned to so many things from my religious past, I still had no interest in reclaiming confession. At the age of twenty-eight, I was even more self-aware of my OCD than I had been in college, and the connection between confession and my obsessions was one that I couldn't forget, or forgive.

Then, about two months after I started dating my husband, we had an intriguing conversation. I hadn't yet disclosed to him my struggles with OCD, but I had told him about those childhood struggles to find confessable actions. He understood; he wasn't a big confession-goer either. "But there was one time when I went to confession, after about ten years away, and it really helped me," he said.

"How?" I asked. "If it's not too personal, I mean."

So he told me that there were two things he had done in his early twenties that weren't consistent with the kind of person he wanted to be. He had tried to acknowledge his regrets and move on, but the actions still weighed him down. Finally, years later, he went to confession and confessed them both. "It really helped," he said. "Hearing the absolution finally gave me closure."

"I can see that," I told him.

"Anyhow," he said, "that's where confession can really be a good thing—when it helps you move on."

Though I didn't know it at the time, the seed was planted. Here was a healthy, balanced man who had been positively touched by confession. It was the first good confession story

I had heard in a long, long time; as such, it made an impression.

I tucked that conversation away in my memory for future pondering.

Months passed. Scott and I became engaged, and our time was taken with wedding plans and marriage preparations. I had come clean with him about my OCD and was getting treatment for it for the first time ever. Thanks to a helpful therapist, I was learning how to let myself off the hook for all of the insignificant things that used to plague me. Looking closely at the thick braid of my life's experiences, I was learning how to identify and separate out the strands of useless guilt. There were quite a few of them.

What was enlightening, though, was that in the process, I discovered some real guilt. Specifically, there was something I had done a few years earlier that I felt truly sorry for. It involved the way I had acted in a past relationship, and I could see how the decision had caused pain and had inhibited my ability to interact fully and authentically with others. Given the chance to go back in time, I realized I would not do it again.

So I sat with my remorse, and then I prayed about it and asked God for forgiveness. But at various happy moments, the memory of my past action would intrude, and I'd instantly feel a heaviness on my soul. *Okay, enough,* I'd tell myself. *Snap out of it. God knows you're sorry.* No luck.

I wondered if this constant guilt was itself just another OCD symptom, but I knew right away that it wasn't. It wasn't guilt that was based on a phantom or on a reimagining of neutral childhood actions. This guilt had its origins in something tangible, in an action that I knew had been wrong for me and other people.

Even so, when the idea of going to confession first popped into mind, I rejected it instantly. For years I had been vociferously opposed to the entire practice, and I was still on strike. But as months passed, I found that I wasn't waving the mental picket sign quite as energetically as before. My husband's positive experience had affected me. Several of my friends started to acknowledge having healing experiences in the confessional. All in all, a kinder, gentler image of confession crept into my consciousness.

As I struggled with this issue, I came to a gradual awareness about the past, the present, and how they could be reconciled. Much of my decision to avoid confession came from a desire to be loyal to my young self and the pain I'd felt. There was no question that the whole Catholic cycle of guilt—of which confession was a part—had hurt me. But as months passed, I came to realize that going back to confession didn't mean that I was denying those childhood memories. I realized that if I were to approach the sacrament with my real, non-fabricated guilt, then I'd be taking the sacrament as it was meant to be taken. It wouldn't dishonor my childhood experiences; rather, it would allow for spiritual freedom in my present.

Gradually, in the deepest part of my soul, the balance was shifting. Finally, one winter day, I realized that it was taking more energy for me to avoid confession than it was for me to go.

All right, I told myself. *It's time.*

On the evening of Ash Wednesday, I made my way to a local church (not the one I attended on Sundays; anonymity felt more appealing to me). I slipped inside the chapel, which was dimly lit. There was a single line of penitents, about four people in all, waiting in front of two confessionals.

For a moment, I felt like I was in grade school again. It all felt instantly familiar: the pall of silence, the sense of nervous import as I stood with eyes fixed above the door, waiting for (literally) the green light to enter and square off with my sins. As I waited, I realized that there were, as of old, two paradoxical feelings tugging at me. There was a desire for the line to move slowly, so as to prolong the moment when I had to come clean, and the wish that it would hurry up so the whole process would be over soon.

I wondered what the priest would be like. Would I be lucky and be greeted by a kind, benevolent presence on the other side of the screen? Or would I be scolded for my absence, or, worse yet, for my sin? Whether kind or gruff, the priest on the left certainly seemed to be the faster of the two; people were leaving his confessional at twice the rate of those on the right side.

The man in front of me entered the confessional on the right. I was the next in line. My heart was pounding, just as it used to. I wondered which priest would finish first. I read the priest's names on the confessionals, but it wasn't my parish, so they meant nothing to me either way.

I waited.

The door to the left-hand confessional opened, and a woman came out.

I went inside and shut the door.

Thanks to a small light on the wall next to the kneeler, there was none of the complete darkness of the confessionals of my memory. I could make out a small crucifix on the wall, and below it the text of the Act of Contrition. I registered all this with a feeling of relief.

Still, kneeling in front of the screen made me suddenly, nervously, aware of the full significance of what I was about to do. I was used to kneeling in Mass, of course, but this was different. Here there was no altar, no Eucharist, nothing beyond myself on which I could focus. There were no visual distractions, just me and my past and my now-urgent need to lay it to rest.

A voice on the other side of the screen said, "In the name of the Father, and of the Son, and of the Holy Spirit, Amen." It caught me off guard; the voice was closer than I expected it to be. It had a slight accent, Irish perhaps. I made the sign of the cross hastily.

"Bless me, Father, for I have sinned," I said. My voice sounded tiny and weak. I was taken aback by how vulnerable I sounded. And then I thought, *But this is a place where I am allowed to sound vulnerable.*

"It's been fifteen years since my last confession," I said, and then stopped, thinking that the priest would wish to comment on my time away. I also paused because I was beginning to choke up. It was suddenly hard for me to speak.

The priest was silent. "Is there a specific sin that has brought you here today?" he asked after a pause.

I told him. It felt good to cry without being seen.

He didn't scold. He didn't ask for details, nor did he seem in any way affected by my sin. He asked if I went to Mass. I told him yes, nearly every Sunday.

"Remember that God comes to you in the Mass, and has been with you always," he responded. He said a few more sentences in that vein, about Christ walking beside me in all moments of my life. They sounded like words he had said often; he rattled them off in a string, dispassionately, almost without pausing.

I continued to cry as he spoke. I tried to focus on his words, but I was distracted by the novelty of crying in a stranger's presence. Even beyond that, I was distracted by the significance of having just revealed the neediest, and therefore most secret, part of myself.

For my penance, he told me to say any prayer that came to me. He didn't ask for an Act of Contrition, which surprised me; I began to understand why his line had moved so quickly. When he absolved me and told me to go in peace, I thanked him and got up. The entire ritual had taken about a minute and a half.

Kneeling in a nearby pew, facing the small altar, I let my mind process the experience. A mix of feelings jumbled in my head. Foremost among them, I recognized that, in spite of my tears, the whole process had felt, well, rather anti-climactic. I'd expected that the priest would be surprised and curious about my journey, but he had sounded dry and mechanical, as if he were just trying to get through the line of penitents before Mass—which, probably, he was.

As I knelt there, a thought flew into my mind. Maybe, somehow, this experience wasn't supposed to be dramatic. After all, I hadn't gone to confession to be forgiven by God. He'd done that long ago. No, this confession was about something else entirely. It was about me forgiving myself.

Nothing else had worked. Although I knew intellectually that God had forgiven me, I needed to do more than just think it. I needed another person's voice to say, "Your sins are forgiven; go in peace." I needed to hear that mercy and resolution come from outside myself.

It's so astonishing that whatever we regret, God will forgive. Who would do that, when we can barely forgive ourselves? It boggles the mind, and if you're like me, my brain alone can't make me believe it. That's why hearing it—hearing the voice of Christ, coming through the lips of another person into my ears—has a power that can't be denied.

The seven sacraments are defined as visible signs of God's grace. I think confession should have an asterisk by it, though, because when it takes place in a darkened box, there is nothing visible about it. When you can't see the person who is administering the sacrament, the sense of hearing alone is what brings the healing. Confession is an *audible* sign of God's grace, and it's one kind of proof that the ears can indeed be pathways to the soul.

As I got up and left the chapel, I felt different. I felt lighter, almost buoyant; I felt free. I experienced the sacrament as it was meant to be experienced—not as a ritual that feeds my anxiety but as one that liberates me from it.

And now, years later, I think about my past and every bit of guilt is gone. I heard what I needed to hear in that dark confessional on Ash Wednesday. I heard forgiveness, and there is no sound more beautiful.

Begin

Take a few slow breaths. Center yourself and open up to feel God's presence. Ask for God's grace as you enter this time of prayerful reflection.

Give thanks

Think about God's endless capacity to forgive. Give thanks for the sacrament that lets us actually hear that forgiveness.

Review

Think of your own confession experiences. Is it a sacrament you participate in often? If so, why? If not, why not?

Think about your own experience of guilt. Do you also have to distinguish between fabricated guilt and the real thing? Are you able to do that effectively? Would it help to involve someone else in the process?

Is there anyone in your life you have wronged and from whom you would love to hear the words "I forgive you"? Is there anyone who may be longing to hear those very same words from you? Pray for a spirit of discernment here.

Look ahead

Find a time to go back to confession, if you don't normally go. If you do go often, pay particular attention to the words of the priest as he grants God's forgiveness. Recognize the voice of Jesus speaking through those words, and let the sound of forgiveness liberate you.

Smell

Take a moment to think of the unique smell of each of these:

- The ocean
- Clean laundry
- A Christmas tree
- Fast-food French fries

How easy was it to recall them? Probably not too hard. In fact, as you reflected upon these individual smells, you may have found other memories coming to mind: the feel of waves against your feet, or the warm air of your laundry room, or a holiday ornament you always put in a place of honor near the top of the Christmas tree, or the brown plastic trays of your local McDonald's.

Smell is often called our most evocative sense. The brain's olfactory cortex, where smells are processed, is situated in the part of the brain where emotional memories are stored. Maybe that's why smell can seem like a hand reaching out of your childhood, pulling you back into an experience you haven't thought about in years. It's a powerful connection to our past.

But an awareness of smells can also illuminate our present. It can help us live more mindfully and gratefully. It can help us recognize that God's goodness saturates the world, in scents that are both obvious and subtle.

11

Smells of Childhood

"I can still remember the smell of the old tin washtub I used to sit in at my grandparents' house," says my seventy-four-year-old dad. "On hot days I'd sit in the tub in their yard in Chicago, and it smelled like galvanized metal. I haven't smelled anything like it in years, but I don't have to because it is a smell I can recall instantly, even now."

"You know what your house smelled like?" asks my childhood friend as we sip wine in my backyard. "It smelled like laundry. I'd go up the front walk to your house, and your mom would have a load of clothes in the dryer in the garage, and that vent from the dryer pumped the air right out onto the walkway, and it smelled like dryer sheets in a blast of warm air. I always think of that smell when I think of your house."

"I remember the smell of lemon trees," says my mom. "When I was twelve we lived in a little hacienda-like house in Santa Barbara, in the middle of a grove of lemon trees. There was a narrow lane going through it. I'd take the bus to school and I had to walk about a mile along the lane. It smelled so pretty walking through there in the afternoon. Our collie dog would run through the lemon groves in the morning when it was damp, and I still remember the smell of his wet fur."

And me? Well, I remember the smell of the umbrella I had when I was seven. It was made of clear vinyl, printed with pictures of Snoopy holding balloons of yellow and green and red. I'd unfurl its clingy folds on a rainy day, and it smelled deliciously toxic, the winter equivalent of the inflatable inner tubes that I'd use in summer. Thirty-five years later, I think of the smell and my childhood comes back in a rush. I feel the curved plastic handle with its finger grips, and I hear the steady patter of drops on the ground, and I remember the odd, fun sensation of looking at the world through a screen of vinyl and a veil of rain and a few backward Snoopys, and I wonder if any of us would be able to remember anything at all without our sense of smell.

Begin

Take a few slow breaths. Center yourself and open up to feel God's presence. Ask for God's grace as you enter this time of prayerful reflection.

Give thanks

Think about the complexity of the human brain, which can recall smells years after they happen. Thank God for the gift of memory, especially the ability to remember the little things that make up a childhood.

Review

Think about smells you associate with your childhood. It may be easiest to imagine a place where you spent a lot of time and think about what it smelled like. Which smells come to mind?

Let yourself sit with one of the memories associated with the smell. What experiences or people do you associate with that smell? How did that experience or those people help shape the person you are today?

As an adult, can you recall a time when you smelled something that immediately took you back to your childhood? What was the smell? Were you surprised by its power to bring the past to your mind?

Look ahead

Pay attention to the smells of the places where you live, work, and spend a lot of your time. What does your home smell like? What does your workplace smell like? Think of the memories that are being stored in your brain, even on the most ordinary day. Can you tell which smells may trigger memories, years from now?

12

Lavender

It was a warm, languid summer afternoon. My two young boys were napping in their rooms, and the house was silent. Relishing the break, I logged on to Facebook, which I'd joined a few weeks earlier. Since then my vocabulary, on which as an English teacher I'd already prided myself as being pretty extensive, had increased significantly. Status updates. Likes. Tagging. "Friend" as a verb.

Facebook was seductively fun, a carnival of my present and my past. In the first few weeks I was online, I reconnected with high school buddies and college acquaintances. My little gallery of online friends, each with a small square picture, was steadily increasing. It was entertaining to click on profiles, peering through the unshuttered online windows into their lives, seeing which friends liked *The Daily Show* or Garth Brooks.

But as the minutes ticked by, I began to feel both overfull and unsatisfied. It was that Halloween-night-I'm-eating-too-much-candy kind of feeling. I didn't really want to be online anymore, but I kept clicking away aimlessly. All the same, getting up from the chair seemed to take too much effort. Scrolling through the images on the screen was the path of least resistance, and I wasn't in a resisting kind of mood.

But I wasn't in a peaceful kind of mood either.

Eventually, I got up from the computer and went to the garage. Pulling out my pruning shears, garden gloves, and a bucket, I took them to the front yard, where a lavender bush grew in the sunlight. I'd planted it a few years earlier, and it had grown to a nice respectable size, its purple spears spreading out in all directions. In the summer warmth, several of the stalks had begun to fade, their blossoms turning to light brown.

As most gardeners know, it's not easy to deadhead lavender. Unlike roses, the sheer number of the stalks makes it an investment of time. Working around the bush, even a medium-sized one, is hardly a quick process.

If I'm making it sound like an onerous task, though, I'm giving a false impression. Deadheading lavender isn't work to me; it's aromatherapy.

As with most scents, lavender is an impossible fragrance to describe in words. When I free-associate, though, I have no lack of things to say: *Clean. Summer. Fields in Provence. English garden. Fresh linen. Bed and breakfast. A lady's soap dish.* It's a purifying scent, one that seems capable of dominating any other smell around it, in a good way. It can overcome murk, sweat, and sour laundry. It can change the mood of a room—or a piece of clothing, or a media-saturated mom—like nothing else.

As I bent over and snipped each stalk, rubbing the blooms between my fingers and feeling a slight (and not unpleasant) residue on my skin, I felt myself growing more and more peaceful. My mind, which had been glutted with photos and graphics and status updates, was being refreshed. It wasn't the click-of-a-key refreshment but a deep refreshment, as if I were opening the windows of my very self to let in clean, sweet air.

As a blogger, I'm the last person to criticize the Internet. But I've found that it's remarkably easy to get seduced into giving it more time than it deserves. Brief two-dimensional glimpses into the faraway lives of other people can sometimes feel more compelling than the concrete life right in front of me, in my very own house and yard. I don't think that's entirely a problem; curiosity about what lies beyond our immediate lives is always a trait worth encouraging. That said, there are times when I find myself spinning my wheels online, not really being edified by what I'm seeing and yet oddly reluctant to leave. It's as if I keep waiting for some update, some little hit, to do what the Internet can't do—to do what only real life can.

Snip. Snip. With the sun on my head, I worked my way around the fragrant lavender, cutting away the thin fibrous stalks, absorbed and happy. The Internet is a feast for the eyes, yes, but I'm more than just a pair of eyes. Sometimes I need a gentle reminder that real life has three dimensions, and real life has a smell.

Begin

Take a few slow breaths. Center yourself and open up to feel God's presence. Ask for God's grace as you enter this time of prayerful reflection.

Give thanks

Take some time to thank God for the smells of the natural world.

Review

Look back over your experiences of nature. What are the positive scents you've encountered there? Maybe lilacs, pine forests, the smell of rain after a summer shower?

Do you ever take time to "stop and smell the lavender"? Why or why not?

Does technology hijack your attention and become your default way to spend your free time? When you do spend time outdoors, does your phone or any other device end up claiming your attention? How do you feel about that?

Look ahead

Find a time when, typically, you would be looking at a screen, and use it to spend some time in nature. Don't just look at what is around you; take a deep breath and smell God's creation. Even if you can't leave home, sit in front of an open window and breathe in the smell of the outdoors.

13

The Odor of the Sheep

A nose is great when it comes to freshly baked cookies, newly washed hair, honeysuckle blossoms, and the cool salty smell of the ocean. When I experience fragrances like these, I think: *I'm so blessed to have the ability to smell. My life would be so impoverished without it. I am finding the goodness of God with every scented breath.*

And then I find myself doing a particularly odiferous task, such as cleaning up vomit or swabbing the toilet. I'm stuck doing something that stinks, figuratively and literally, and I find myself breathing through my mouth and envying friends of mine who have colds.

So where is God in this? Where is God in the odors that make us feel sick and the smells that make us want to exit a room at top speed?

If I'm truly Ignatian about this, I have to believe that God is found in those moments too. I don't think it's just about suffering or "offering it up," about training ourselves to endure, even though there is arguably something worthy about learning to do so.

I think these bad smells have something to teach us about humanity and thus about compassion. They provide a kind of conscience tweak, a reminder that the people who generate these odors are just as worthy of dignity as their more deliciously fragrant counterparts. Because if we learn nothing else from the example of Jesus Christ, we should believe this: whether we smell like roses or like urine, every one of us matters.

This is not an easy lesson, maybe because we live in a world where offending someone's nostrils is a major social faux pas. Most of us can't imagine life without deodorant, toothpaste, frequent showers, and breath mints. And it's fair to say that nothing creates a buffer around you like a bad odor. The only empty seats on a busy bus are usually the ones next to the person who smells like urine or excrement or sour unwashed clothing; many of us would rather stand than take the adjoining seat. An affront to the sense of smell feels instinctive; it is hard to intellectualize it, to look past it.

And yet there are people among us who, day after day, do the jobs that stink. I think of day-care providers, who change countless diapers. Or custodians, who clean out rank toilets and garbage cans. Nurses and doctors are no strangers to the worst odors a body can produce. And nearly every parent can relate to the experience of a vomit episode that leaves you breathless (particularly when it happens in the confined space of a car).

How long does it take someone in these jobs to develop an impassivity to these odors? How long before they can avoid instinctively covering their noses and can manage to maintain a neutral expression—or, even better, a deeply compassionate one? Because even if our flesh recoils from these smells, on the other end of these stinky jobs is usually a human being in need, someone who is young, old, homeless, ill, vulnerable. And to really see the person behind the smell is what Jesus would do—and what we're all called to do as well.

In one of his oft-quoted homilies, Pope Francis made the observation that pastors should have "the odor of the sheep."

He doesn't say they should smell the sheep once and then leave for more fragrant company. He says they should smell *like* them, which implies sticking around them for a while. It's like what happens when I leave my favorite café after two hours of grading papers. I come home, and my hair and clothing carry the unmistakable smell of coffee beans, so much so that my husband can immediately tell where I've been.

Pope Francis's words are a helpful way to think about our relationship with the vulnerable and marginalized. He invites us to hang out with them so often and so long that we take on some of their attributes. He challenges us to stay there so long that others will be able to identify the company we've kept.

And if we ourselves begin to smell like the marginalized, we are changed in profound ways. We move through the world knowing how it feels when others cover their noses at our approach. We experience the world as the ill or old or homeless or rejected do, and we know how it feels when others turn away with martyred or outraged expressions, when they give us a wide berth, when they hold themselves deliberately distant, inside a buffer of their personal comfort.

There is a value in all acts of service, but it is true that service feels different when it comes from a place of true empathy. In this way, these bad smells, these jobs that stink, are opportunities for us to start pulling down barriers in this world of many walls. They allow us to smell like the people on the fringes, to know what it means to be on the receiving end of disgust and derision. And they make us all the more grateful for the Christ-like person who knows how we smell but sits down next to us anyway, deliberately sharing our space.

Begin

Take a few slow breaths. Center yourself and open up to feel God's presence. Ask for God's grace as you enter this time of prayerful reflection.

Give thanks

Thank God for the people who serve others, even when it is unpleasant to do so. Offer gratitude for the quality of empathy and the people who are able to put themselves in others' shoes and see the world through their eyes.

Review

Think of times when your service for others has literally stunk. How did you react? Did you complain, or did you help them with good grace?

Make a mental list of people who have helped you, especially with the smelly and unpleasant tasks. They may be people you have encountered personally or those who are unknown to you (those who clean the bathrooms at the mall or who empty your garbage cans).

Think of a person or group of people from whom you tend to keep your distance, a group on the margins. Why are you reluctant to engage with them? What can you do to change that in the future?

Look ahead

Tomorrow, offer to do an unpleasant, possibly stinky task. Don't ask for recognition; instead, keep your focus on the human beings you are helping by doing so. Recognize them as people of dignity.

14

Candle Smoke

Prayer candles in a church have an evocative beauty all their own. The metal candleholders are dotted with plocks of wax and half-burned matchsticks lie at angles in the tray below. The candles themselves are sometimes small and stubby, banded with aluminum; others are taller and more statuesque, enclosed in glass. Lighting one involves a familiar ritual: the hunt for a usable match, the transfer of fire from an already burning candle to the match tip, then the tiny flare as the wick of the new candle welcomes the flame. Then the prayer begins, and the candle burns as long as it can until it goes out. This ritual is in the Catholic blood; Father Andrew Greeley once quipped, "A rule of thumb: if there are no votive candles in it, a church really isn't Catholic."

Even aside from prayer candles, fire has a strong presence in every Catholic church. Candles glow on or near the altar during each celebration of the Mass. The red sanctuary lamp burns whenever the tabernacle holds the consecrated hosts. Every Easter the huge Paschal candle is lit, the light of new life piercing the darkness of death. And where there's fire, there's eventually smoke as well.

Like incense, candle smoke is one of the primary ingredients that make up that distinctively delicious church smell. Unlike liturgical incense, though, smoke is not church-specific. It shows up in what we might call secular life as well, its pungent scent the common link between all kinds of different memorable events.

In my life, smoke shows up anytime we celebrate a birthday and a friend or family member makes a wish over the candles on a cake. Smoke is often the scent of date night, coming from a votive candle on a restaurant table or from a candle on the dresser. In my house, smoke rises to my nose after a session at the prayer desk in my bedroom, where I light a candle to usher in a period of silence at the end of a busy day. Smoke can be a sign of prayer or a sign of celebration. Often, it's both at the same time. It's a smell that helps me recognize the holiness in life outside of the walls of a church—which is, of course, where I spend the vast majority of my time.

This truth hit home in a big way for me last Advent when, for the first time, I attempted to do a weekly Advent wreath ceremony with the kids. It wasn't the easiest time to start a weekly liturgical ritual; December was as chaotic as December usually is, doubly so with the end of my teaching semester and stacks of papers to grade. Gathering the family right before the boys' bedtime on a Sunday night took a certain amount of effort, but I was determined. *We could use some Advent prayer,* I thought. *Other families get a lot of meaning out of this. Let's make it happen.*

All the ingredients were in place: a booklet of prayers and reflections, a circular holder displaying four candles on the dining-room table, a lighter, all four family members gathered together. The boys sat on their knees on chairs, waiting expectantly. Everyone looked at me to begin, and I suddenly found that I had no idea what to do. This isn't like praying the rosary, where you have a specific formula to follow. I thought that there was probably some right way to do an Advent wreath, and I really didn't know what it was.

But I went for it and lit the candle. The boys, wearing their fleecy pajamas, rested their elbows on the table and sat staring at the flame. I attempted to read a few words from the

Advent booklet, which was hard to do in the near dark. My older son asked to read it himself; I handed him the book, and he stumbled over some of the words but read gamely on as the candle flickered and wavered and we all stood or sat around our table.

It was nice, being together like that. We went around the table, each person sharing one thing he or she wanted to do that week: follow directions, pray more, think more about Jesus, and so on. And I realized that what mattered more than the words was the fact that we were all together, looking at the same wavering flame, each of us lost in the presence of something glowing and beautiful. It was a prayer but also a celebration of our little family, however imperfect and ragged our spirituality.

After a few moments had passed and we were done, the boys blew out the candle. One quick blast of breath and smoke curled upward, making all the crazy paths into the air that smoke tends to do. The smell rose to our noses: sharp, dark, unmistakable, familiar.

"It smells like a birthday!" my younger son said happily.

He's right. Candles, when extinguished, basically all smell the same, and they don't smell like anything else. Whether you are blowing out a prayer candle or a candle on a cake, you end up with exactly the same evocative scent.

I love that about candle smoke, how it drifts over the boundaries between the secular and the sacred, obscuring them and reminding us that everyday life is also holy. Its smell is a witness to all the little celebrations, the pauses from our normal routine that we work into our overfull lives. That pause might be a prayer in a quiet church or a Mass that has just ended or the sacred beauty of the Easter Vigil. But candle smoke is also the smell of a long-delayed Valentine's Day dinner between two parents when the kids are finally in bed, or of a Halloween jack-o-lantern once the evening's festivities are done. It's the smell of four family members gathering together to do a faith ritual they aren't entirely sure they know how to do but which somehow turns out to be exactly right.

Begin

Take a few slow breaths. Center yourself and open up to feel God's presence. Ask for God's grace as you enter this time of prayerful reflection.

Give thanks

Thank God for the warmth and light of fire. Reflect on the fact that we practice our faith everywhere, not just within the walls of a church.

Review

Think of occasions that call for the lighting of candles. At church? At home? In other places?

Ponder celebrations that happen in the home—maybe some your family held when you were a child and others you hold now. Where do you find God in them?

Do you invite prayer and faith into your life at home? In what specific ways do you do that?

What prayer or faith rituals might you want to add to your daily routine at home?

Look ahead

Find a place at home to light a candle and pray. If you live with others, invite them into the prayer. At the end of the prayer, blow out the candle and let the smell of the smoke be a part of the prayer, a fragrant witness to the holiness within the walls of your own home.

15

Chrism

When my boys were babies, they—like most infants—were very much in demand. Friends and family members would reach out, eager to hold them. They'd snuggle the boys and breathe their wonderful baby smell and surrender them reluctantly.

On the day each boy was baptized, the magnetic pull was even stronger. I'd like to say it was because of the waves of holiness emanating from their newly splashed little bodies, but, in fact, it was something else. It was the smell of chrism, the holy oil traced on their foreheads by the priests.

"I love this smell," friends and family members kept saying. Holding Matthew or Luke at the baptism party we had for each of the boys, the eager baby holder would stick her nose close to my boy's shiny little forehead and breathe in great gulps. "I wish they made a perfume of this," one friend said, drinking it in as if the only oxygen in the room were an inch from my child's forehead.

Chrism is one of those things that, as Catholics, we don't smell all that often. It's not like incense or candle smoke. You smell it only if you happen to be lucky enough to be at a baptism or a confirmation or the reception of Holy Orders. It's a smell that is hard to classify. Looking at the amber oil in the vial, you would expect it to smell rich or buttery, like really good olive oil. In fact, the chrism I know is almost spicy, rather like incense; I swear there are hints of mint in it too.

Whatever else it is, it's unique, and—in my random sampling of acquaintances—very popular. And though you don't get to smell it very often, it's a scent that lingers.

With both boys, I was reluctant to bathe them after their baptism experiences. I hated to think of that intoxicating scent going away. I need not have worried, because those scent molecules are the olfactory equivalent of burrs: they stick. Days later, the scent of chrism was still there, on their dark little heads. Weeks later, it was still there in their blankets and car seats. Had either of them committed infant crimes on his baptism day, the police would have tracked him down in a second. It was astonishing, the extent to which the scent lingered; it was also very nice.

And it was symbolic because it seemed to say something about the effect of the baptism on my sons. By becoming Catholic, my boys were different in some way from the persons they were before. They had become part of a tribe that was larger than themselves. Baptism connected them to my husband and me, and to friends and family, and to Catholics through the centuries, including lots of my favorite saints, the people who inspire me and whom I hoped would one day inspire my kids. Baptism meant that the Holy Spirit had touched their souls, and although that is not some magical super-hero shield that makes everything in their lives perfect and easy, it was, I hoped, the first step in claiming a faith identity that would make their lives richer and would one day enrich the lives of others through them.

The effects of baptism are not there one day and gone the next. It's an identity that lingers, that stays and cannot easily be forgotten.

I wanted this identity for them because I have seen what a lived Catholic faith can do. Throughout my life, particularly as an adult, I have witnessed Catholics whose faith was the equivalent of the chrism on my boys' foreheads. It captured my attention. It drew me in. It made me want to stay close to those people, as if to absorb some of their essence.

Some such people I know personally. One was the priest who married Scott and me, one of the priests serving at the Stanford Catholic Community when I first began going there. He was in his thirties when I came, and his thoughtful homilies and rich singing voice—he actually sang the Eucharistic prayer, not as a chant but as a beautiful evocative melody—helped me realize that there was something profoundly meaningful in this faith I thought I had rejected.

Others were Mary and Trish, two women I met in my twenties. They were good friends who shared a cramped apartment in San Francisco, an apartment that seemed to expand during their frequent parties. At those parties, conversations often turned to faith, but it wasn't dry faith divorced from life. All struggles were acknowledged and challenges were accepted. They could even joke about faith, proving that a Catholic identity and quirky, fun-loving personalities are not mutually exclusive. Faith was evident in their job choices, in their respective weddings, and in their interactions with everyone they met.

Other inspiring Catholics are people I don't know personally and won't in this life. High on my list is Father Mychal Judge, the Franciscan priest who was the fire chaplain for the

NYFD and lost his life when he rushed to the Twin Towers on 9/11. Biographies of his life paint a picture of a man who was gregarious and adventurous, a recovered alcoholic with an awareness of his own wounds who turned that wound-edness into empathy and love. He knew the homeless by name and counted them as friends, so much so that some of them listed him as their next of kin. He also ministered lovingly to AIDs patients, even in the earliest days of the epidemic when others were terrified to go near them. A life like that, in which a person pours himself out for others, stepping over the chasms that exist between him and those around him—that kind of life draws me.

I see such individuals and I think, *What makes these people so fascinating? What makes them so compassionate, creative, wise, and strong?* I want to breathe their air; I want that fragrance of holiness to rub off on me so that I can live a life like theirs. I want to draw closer to the source of that goodness, just as we bend in to drink in the smell of that chrism. And it makes me hope that somehow I'm managing to be the same for someone else.

Baptism is a big fragrant deal, but it's really just the beginning of a life of faith. As we grow older, we face multiple decision points each day, questions about how to treat others or how to spend our time and attention. The questions just get more complicated the older we become; it can be hard to discern the best way to live.

But any time we attend a baptism, that spicy, delicious chrism can bring us back in touch with a truth worth remembering. It reminds us that few things are more attractive than a life that smells like faith, and like love.

Begin

Take a few slow breaths. Center yourself and open up to feel God's presence. Ask for God's grace as you enter this time of prayerful reflection.

Give thanks

Thank God for the faith community in which you now live. Give thanks for those communities or churches of your past that have brought you to where you are today. If you are not currently active in a faith community, give thanks for the hunger you have that has brought you to this prayer.

Review

Recall baptisms you've attended. Remember the fragrance of the chrism.

Think of people you know whose faith you find attractive. What is it about them that invites others to a similar way of living?

Think of people you don't know whose faith has inspired you. Try to identify what, exactly, attracts you to their life stories.

Look at your spiritual walk from the perspective of someone else. What can that person infer about your faith from your actions? Do you live your faith in such a way that people want to be near it?

Look ahead

Think of how you can project your faith more joyfully. You might strive to be more Christ-like in interactions with others, or discuss your beliefs with someone who is interested, or show that you are happy while attending Mass. Imagine your faith as a scent, and make it an inviting one.

Touch

What are you touching right now?

Most likely you're touching the pages of this book or the electronic device on which you're reading it. But other things are touching you too: clothes against your skin, glasses on your nose, hair brushing your neck. Maybe you feel the hardness of a bus seat or the softness of a sofa. Perhaps the sun is touching your skin, or your child is pulling on your arm, or the family cat is rubbing against your ankle.

"I'm not a touchy-feely person," many of us say, yet there's no escaping touch. Unlike the other senses, which have one primary body part associated with each of them, touch is a full-body experience. We use this sense constantly; it's part of being human.

Jesus, God incarnate, was the same. The feel of sun, wind, water, his mother's lap, clothing, comfortable things, painful things—Jesus was no stranger to any of these sensations. And yet it can be hard to believe this. Jesus can be more comfortable to us as an airy abstract concept, not as a man with a body that felt what we feel.

In the next five chapters, let's take some time to focus on this sense. Let's think about how it relates to love, to prayer, and to comfort. And let's think about Jesus not as an abstraction but as a real man who was not afraid to touch and be touched.

16

The Rosary

Prayer can be hard to pin down, both literally and figuratively. It usually involves words, thoughts, and feelings; there's nothing concrete to it. As a concept, it can sometimes seem downright mysterious.

But for a kid in Catholic school, it was clear and concrete. Prayer was something you held on to—quite literally—when you prayed the rosary.

During our second-grade year at St. Simon's, every child in my class received a plastic rosary. The boys got royal blue, the color of our uniforms, while the girls got a lovely powder blue. I adored that rosary, and though I haven't seen it in years, I still remember the feel of the beads, small and hard, each with a palpable seam of plastic around the circumference. On my rosary, the bottom half of the crucifix listed oddly to the side; you could never actually crucify someone on a cross that askew. The rosary came in a small vinyl case with a flap that folded over to close it, and the beads fit inside perfectly, with no room to spare. The economy of that was very satisfying to me.

Periodically we prayed the rosary in class, following along with the Our Father, ten Hail Marys and the occasional Glory Be. As Catholic as my school was, the rosary was not a daily ritual, and although I loved the physical feel of the beads, I was fine with that. The practice became repetitive, and even though we were supposed to meditate on events in Christ's life as we prayed, I was more likely to be staring at the cinderblock walls than imagining Jesus carrying his cross along a dusty, sunbaked road in Palestine.

I saved that rosary for years, in a small music box that was itself in a shoe box where I kept other childhood treasures. I didn't use it at all during high school that I recall. In college I was doing almost nothing that was particularly Catholic, certainly not the rosary, so decades passed without my praying this way. I did pick up a bright green rosary at the Stanford Catholic Center as I was reengaging with the faith; it seemed like a good thing to have on hand, just as I might pick up duct tape or safety pins. I didn't do anything with it for a few years.

Then, on September 12, 2001, I took it out and prayed it.

It is odd to realize that the high-school students I teach have no memory of September 11 or the terrifying days afterward. I still feel it viscerally, the shock and horror of that day and the constant, unrelenting tragedy that unfolded on the news, each frame worse than the last. I remember the footage of the second plane striking the tower, and the shocked newscasters who were at a loss for words. I still see the missing-persons fliers posted together around Ground Zero, a desperate quilt, each square another family's tragedy. One young woman and her brother, searching for their father, are burned in my memory. She was able to speak relatively calmly to the reporter while her brother stood at her side, his mouth in a crooked line of emotion, clamped shut as if he feared that opening it even the slightest bit would be his undoing. I had never seen anything like that day. I guess none of us had.

And, like most of us, I had to do something. I found the green rosary, sat cross-legged on the bed, and held each bead tightly, praying while the mountain of damp Kleenex by my side grew steadily larger.

It was not a magic formula or talisman that made every-thing better, but it did help. It was something I could hold on to, literally. Little in life seemed certain that day. Things we all had thought were solid as steel could be toppled. As a native Californian, I think immediately of an earthquake analogy: the ground has moved, and is still moving, and at this moment, you desire nothing more than to grab hold of something solid.

Those beads were solid. They were tangible proof that there was something other than my own fear in the room. There was my desire to pray; there was also, I believed, some-one hearing that prayer. More than any other prayer I prayed that day, the rosary helped.

Even on less desperate days, I still sometimes reach for my rosary. I don't always pray it as it is meant to be prayed, med-itating on the mysteries. Sometimes I think of an intention for each bead and state it to God, holding that person or that crisis in my mind and in my fingers for a moment before let-ting go and moving on to the next bead. Some evenings I just play with it, listening to the faint sounds of the beads as they click softly against one another. Other times I wind the rosary around my hand and savor the comforting feel of it that way, as if the prayer is holding me together on days when I fear I might fall to pieces.

I am not sure why it works exactly, except that it serves to concentrate my prayer and my focus. It gives weight to my prayer, on a few different levels. The rosary brings my faith down to earth. It keeps me in touch with things I need to remember.

Thinking back to my grad-school days, I believe there was something prescient about my decision to pick up that free green rosary. I don't pray with it every day, but having a rosary in the house is somewhat like having that little bitty screwdriver or that roll of painters' tape: when I need it, I really need it. I need it on days when my attention wanders, and it helps me remember where to direct my prayers. I also need it on those scary days when life as I knew it is gone and I feel terrifyingly unmoored, like a balloon with a broken string, not sure where I'll end up. In that string of beads lies one of the paradoxes of prayer: sometimes, the best way to rise above your fear is to hold tight, and to keep on holding.

Begin

Take a few slow breaths. Center yourself and open up to feel God's presence. Ask for God's grace as you enter this time of prayerful reflection.

Give thanks

Take a moment to reflect upon your faith and all the times it has given you something to hold on to. Give thanks for faith that can help us navigate the hardest times.

Review

Consider your own experiences of the rosary. Is it currently a part of your prayer life? Why or why not?

Have you ever prayed holding on to something else—a prayer stone, a crucifix, someone else's hand? What were those experiences like for you?

When you are most in distress, how do you pray? Does it help to hold on to something solid?

Look ahead

Try praying while holding on to something. It could be a rosary, or a piece of jewelry, or something that relates to the person or situation you are praying for. If it's a rosary, don't feel that you always need to pray with it in the traditional way. Try identifying one intercession or bit of gratitude for each bead. See how having something to hold changes the experience of praying.

17

Madonna and Child

In some pictures, the mother and baby are blond; in others, they are brunette. Some artists paint them in royal robes, while others clothe them in rustic peasant dress. The background varies: the mother holds her child in a grassy field, in a darkened room, or against a backdrop of gold leaf.

She holds the baby differently in each painting. In some, he is seated squarely on her lap, sitting upright, while in others she holds him firmly to her heart. Though the nature of the embrace varies, it's always there. The hairstyles or clothing or skin color or background may change, but touch is the common link uniting thousands of images of Madonna and Child. It's one of the most beloved—perhaps the most beloved—subjects of Western art.

On a primal level, this image resonates. We've all been there, in that embrace. Even if we aren't parents ourselves, we know deep in our memory that at one time we were held like that, closely, by someone who cared for us and nurtured us, someone for whom holding us felt as natural as breathing. These images, in all their variety and universality, demonstrate that touch is a major witness to love.

When my kids were babies, they were often in my arms. I remember the feel of their tiny bodies and their damp heads, the little fists that would grab at hair or earrings, the sight of their intent gaze inches from my face, unaffected by society's prohibition against staring at another person at close range. It was a time when my kids were easy to pick up and grab, when they didn't run off on their own. So much of what I valued and loved was there in my arms. It was hard sometimes, juggling baby, car keys, and purse, and yet my arms wanted to hold them. Picking them up at day care felt, in a simple word, good; I loved the weight of them draped over my shoulder, like a bag of sand in a Carter's sleeper.

It's a powerful expression of love, that Madonna-like embrace. Above and beyond that, I've found that touch has a creative power as well. Motherhood has shown me that touch can intensify and build upon a feeling that is already present, making it stronger than it was before.

When my first son was born, I adored him instantly with a kind of love I had never known before. But along with joy and discovery, the first few days of motherhood presented many new challenges. Between the lack of sleep, the wildly fluctuating postpartum hormones, and the difficulties of recovering from a C-section, I began to worry that I wasn't bonding with Matthew as quickly as I should.

A few days after we returned home from the hospital, I opened up and told my mom what I was thinking. "I love him so much, but at times I feel like he's this little stranger in my life."

"In a way, he is a stranger," said my wise mother. "You've just met him. It will take time to get to know him."

A day or two later, after dinner, I sat on the sofa with my baby son. I propped my feet up on the edge of the coffee table, making a slanted deckchair out of my bent legs, and I rested Matthew there. His tiny body sat in my lap with his back against my thighs. I can still picture the sleeper he was wearing, which was decorated with small blue polka dots and red, orange, and yellow vehicles. A CD of lullabies played in the background, and I just sat there, holding my sweet little boy and smoothing his sleek dark hair and letting his tiny fists close around my fingers. I gently moved my body and his in time to the music. In that half hour that I held him—not to feed him or change him or burp him, but just to hold him—I could feel him becoming a stranger no more. It was one of the most beautiful and precious experiences of my life.

I wonder how many other moms have a similar story, the experience of holding their new baby and feeling the relationship deepen through that simple experience of touch. Was this the same process by which Mary came to know her newborn son? Was this how she came to bond with him, to fully grow into her surprising and dizzying new role? Perhaps the more she held him, the more she felt the desire to hold him, to drape him gently over her shoulder or prop him against her bent knees or hold him close to her heart.

However it happened for Mary, there's no question that these Madonna and Child portraits transcend time, always relevant no matter what else changes. In the end, I think these images resonate with us because they affirm the powerful relationship between touch and love. Holding a child means becoming an armchair, letting your body do what your heart does: surround your child with affection. It is a powerful thing to be the one who gives that embrace—powerful, too, to be the one who receives it.

And I'm no theologian, but when I look at those pictures and remember that the baby on the mother's lap is the

Almighty, it makes me understand the Incarnation in an entirely new way. I don't know why God chose to enter the world as an infant; there are many possible reasons, I'm sure. But I like to think that maybe it's because God, too, wanted to feel the warmth of a mother's touch.

Begin

Take a few slow breaths. Center yourself and open up to feel God's presence. Ask for God's grace as you enter this time of prayerful reflection.

Give thanks

Ponder the people who have raised you and held you. Give thanks for their role in your life.

Review

Think of images of the Madonna and Child that you have seen. What feelings do these pictures bring up for you? Do you find yourself identifying more with Mary or with Jesus?

Think of people throughout your life whose touch has been healing or affirming. Think of how that touch has built love or in some way helped your well-being.

Think of the past twenty-four hours. Whom did you touch, and why?

Look ahead

The next time you embrace someone, do it intentionally. Whether hugging a friend, kissing a child good-bye at school, or shaking a colleague's hand, be conscious of the action and make it a way to communicate your goodwill or love for the other person.

18

Comfort

Many people are familiar with the term *comfort food*. It's the food you turn to on a hard day when you just want to feel good about yourself (and it usually involves carbs, sugar, or Mom's recipes).

In a similar vein, I'd like to introduce two new terms to our vocabulary: *comfort clothes* and *comfort furniture*.

When I'm feeling tired/stressed/ill/depressed, I can tell you exactly what I'll be wearing: black yoga pants, a long knit shirt, and fuzzy slippers. I can tell you exactly where I want to be: in bed, that cozy nest that, after years, has been molded to my shape. If it's not bedtime, my favorite place to be is the wingback chair that once belonged to my grandfather, a chair in which I can comfortably rest my head and where I feel safe, surrounded by upholstery and love.

Some things just feel good, period. We go to them when we want comfort.

Parents see this with their kids all the time. Whether it's a blankie or a favorite stuffed animal that eventually becomes filthy with love, some items simply feel good to hold. One of my sons, as an infant, was in the habit of pulling off one of his tiny socks and stroking it against his face. He loved the feel of the soft fuzziness against his cheek. (I'd never try this with my own socks, but then, I guess baby feet—like almost everything else on a baby—are sweeter than their adult counterparts.)

At times our attachment to comfort items can create problems. My sister, Amy, had a beloved blanket when she was a baby and toddler, and when my family went on vacation to Yosemite, Blankie was of course an honored guest. All was fine until the family left the lodge to go on a hike, then came back to find that Blankie had vanished without a trace. My parents' only theory was that the housekeeper had seen it, thought it was one of her old rags, and chucked it in with the other laundry. My sister's anguished screams echoed around the valley, and my parents ended up at Lost and Found writing out a description of the missing item ("Threadbare yellow blanket with pink and blue elephant print"). Amy calmed down only after my mother promised to take her to the fabric store immediately upon the return home to pick out Blankie the Second.

I might pitch the same kind of fit if someone ever took my yoga pants.

But that's the nature of human beings: we become attached to things that are nice to the touch. When we need emotional comfort, we want something that feels physically soothing against our skin. And I don't think this is a bad thing, other than in situations such as the cautionary tale above (which, parents, is proof that you should always take Blankie on the hike with you).

All this gets me thinking about God. Where does God fit into my hierarchy of Comforting Things? Is God a source of comfort for me? Is God the divine equivalent of that soft bed into which I can burrow and feel, eventually, renewed?

Sometimes he is, and other times he isn't. In my weak moments, God feels more like an iron figure with severe planes and pointy corners. Perhaps I'm the victim of bad theology somewhere along the line, but as much as I believe in a loving and merciful God, there are still times when God seems more like the judge, the stern boss-man, the big heavy door that swings shut in my face and doesn't permit me to enter. In the lightning storms of life, God sometimes feels more like Captain von Trapp with his whistle than like Maria with her soft safe bed and her comforting song. That can't be right.

I'm not going to deny that there is something awesome and amazing and bigger-than-I-can-fathom about God. As someone once observed, if we could understand God, then what we are understanding would not be God. Yet, when I think about terms such as *awesome* and *amazing* in relation to the divine, I tend to assume that they apply to the aspects of God that are majestic and powerful. I need to remind myself that maybe the characteristics of God that are bigger than I can comprehend are also the softer, more comforting ones. I need to understand that God is fathomless depths, all right, but those depths are soothing ones too.

Maybe on those tough days when nothing seems to be going right, I can challenge myself to add a little something to my yoga pants, slippers, and pillow routine. I can take a moment to feel the divine presence enveloping me with warmth. I can ditch any residual echo of God as the metal folding chair and sink into the reality of God as the soft lap, comforting me in both body and soul.

Begin

Take a few slow breaths. Center yourself and open up to feel God's presence. Ask for God's grace as you enter this time of prayerful reflection.

Give thanks

Pray your thanks for the things that feel comforting on a hard day. Take a moment to feel grateful for a creator God who gave us the ability to be healed through touch.

Review

When you were a child, what comfort object did you love? Was it a blankie, a stuffed animal, a doll? Why did you love that particular thing?

In your life today, what things are comforting to touch? Think of the clothes you wear on a hard day, a favorite piece of furniture, or blankets or sheets that feel particularly cozy. Remember specific times when they have soothed you.

Do you struggle to see God as a source of comfort? Do you know why or why not?

Look ahead

Find a comfortable blanket. Wrap yourself in it. Breathe slowly and deeply. Imagine that the blanket is God, surrounding you with warmth and love.

19

Water

It's a hot summer afternoon in our backyard. The little blue wading pool is full, and my kids are standing in the cold water, which hits them halfway between ankle and knee. They amuse themselves by fishing with a plastic fishing rod, sailing small boats, and filling random assorted plastic containers to water my flowers. Later they ask me to turn on the rotating sprinkler, and I attach it to the hose and set it in the middle of the lawn. They step away, rock back and forth a bit on their feet in anticipation, then run through the fan-shaped stream of water as it bends slowly forward. It looks so inviting on this sweltering day that I run through it too. It's a shock, the coolness of the water from our hose, but it refreshes me.

It reminds me of all those summer days when *I* was a kid, when my mom would turn on the backyard sprinklers and my sister and I would run through them. On other hot days, we'd be invited to the home of a friend with a pool. It was so exciting, that plunge into the aquamarine water and the instantaneous, welcoming shift from hot to cold.

Drinking water is essential for life, of course, and yet there is something about the *feel* of water that seems just as important. It's a welcome relief, something that seems almost miraculous in its power to refresh and restore. My freshman year of college, it did not rain until months after the start of school, which is typical of Southern California weather patterns. My roommate, who was from Seattle, missed the damp climate she had always known. As soon as the first drops began to fall, she went outside and danced in the rain, greeting it like an old friend.

In Psalm 63:1 the psalmist writes, "O God, you are my God, I seek you, my soul thirsts for you; my flesh faints for you, as in a dry and weary land where there is no water." It's not just the inside of our bodies that needs water. Our skin craves it too, to cleanse and cool and calm.

Perhaps this is why water plays such a significant role in our Catholic lives. We have the sacrament of baptism, of course, that outpouring of water and the Spirit. There's also holy water, into which we reflexively dip our fingers as we enter or leave a church. At our parish there is a large container of holy water by the office door; parishioners are free to bring their own bottles or containers and fill them, to take them home for their own domestic fonts or blessings. DO NOT DRINK says the sign nearby, and I like that the sign is there. It affirms that water plays multiple roles and does more than just assuage thirst. It reminds us that water also has the power to restore us from the outside in.

If you're like me, though, you take this life force very much for granted. In America we expect clean water to be there any time we turn on the tap; if it isn't, we're indignant, as if a fundamental human right has been revoked. When water is scarce, it is dedicated to drinking, not to bathing or cooling off, and our skin misses it. Here in California, we are in the throes of a record-breaking drought, with mandatory water restrictions. We are fortunate that we have all the drinking water we need, but the ability to lounge in the shower for long periods or to put on the sprinklers simply for fun has been severely curtailed. Those days when my boys would point the hose straight up in the air and let the water fall back down on their heads, a kind of backyard blessing, are now something we can't do at all, or can do only furtively with guilt. Like everyone in the state, I'm hoping for a wet winter and spring to restore and refresh this parched landscape.

There is something about water that we can't do without. It's elemental, essential. Maybe that's why it is so fitting that in one of the Eucharistic prayers of the Mass, the priest calls God "the fount of all holiness" and asks the Lord to send down his spirit "like the dewfall." There is no better way to capture the essence of God than in the pure coolness that bathes our bare feet as we walk over the lawn in the morning, in the fountain that fills our cupped palms and still keeps on flowing.

Begin

Take a few slow breaths. Center yourself and open up to feel God's presence. Ask for God's grace as you enter this time of prayerful reflection.

Give thanks

Water is something we tend to take for granted. Pause to thank God for water, for the ease with which we have it, and for the cleanliness of our water system.

Review

Think of all the ways you've used water in the past twenty-four hours. Reflect upon the various ways it supports your existence and makes it better.

Recall a time when the touch of water on your skin was particularly welcome. Try to pinpoint the positive effect it had on you. Let yourself feel that feeling again.

Are there places in your spiritual life that feel dry and parched? What might refresh them?

Look ahead

The next time you shower, wash, or swim, do so with more focus on the experience. Reflect on the feel of water as a gift, not as a given. Pray for those who live in places where water is scarce or unclean. If you can, consider donating to organizations that help bring clean water to people who need it.

20

The Woman in Luke 7

One of the Pharisees asked Jesus to eat with him, and he went into the Pharisee's house and took his place at the table. And a woman in the city, who was a sinner, having learned that he was eating in the Pharisee's house, brought an alabaster jar of ointment. (Luke 7:36–37)

To reflect on this story, we have to imagine the backstory of the unnamed woman. She has no other identity within this story than that of "sinner"; it's a label that the Pharisee quickly recognizes and seems to see as her only identifying feature. The Gospel doesn't specify her sin, but in the context of the time, it surely had something to do with sex.

And if her sin had something to do with sex, then that means it had something to do with touch.

When I think of this mystery woman, I wonder how all of this began for her. Was there one man she loved way back, a man who showed her the pleasure of touching and being touched? And then perhaps it all fell apart from there. The man, who for some reason was unavailable or unwilling to enter into marriage, moved on and would no longer acknowledge her. Word got out; her reputation was gone. She had crossed a line and there was no going back. The only option for her was to touch and be touched by other men, perhaps for money, because the people in her community could not imagine her capable of doing anything else.

Her life was defined by her sin. As she walked through town, women would gossip and turn their backs. Men would look at her in a certain way. They would mutter furtive comments to her under their breath, things that hurt. Sexuality would be the filter through which every man interacted with her, even though she longed for it to be otherwise.

And then she saw Jesus and recognized something entirely different.

I like to imagine that she had seen him before this story. She may have been on the fringes of a crowd, watching him move through the city preaching and healing. Perhaps she and Jesus made eye contact, and she saw in his eyes something she did not see in the appraising or hungry eyes of the other men in her town. She saw something that gave her the courage to show up that day, uninvited, at the home of one of the men in town most likely to publicly judge and shame her.

She no longer wanted to be trapped by her past. But how could she lay that desire in front of another person? How could she communicate the shame, the guilt, the woundedness, the vulnerability, the desire to make human contact with the one person who would see her not for her sin, but for her truest self?

She didn't say it with words. She said it with touch.

She stood behind him at his feet, weeping, and began to bathe his feet with her tears and to dry them with her hair. Then she continued kissing his feet and anointing them with the ointment (7:38).

Touch has caused problems for her in the past. It has been a key player in all those encounters she's come to regret. And yet she doesn't shy away from it here. She does not swing so far in the other direction that she ends up rejecting something that is, by its very nature, good. She is reclaiming touch.

Her touch here is not sexual, but it is intimate. She is putting her whole body into it: hands, hair, and lips. It must be an astonishing thing to witness. And she is using touch as it is meant to be used, not as a means of cheapening others but as a way to show love and to communicate our most essential selves. Sometimes touch is the only way to communicate those things, because words can fail and some emotion goes too deep for speech.

Now when the Pharisee who had invited him saw it, he said to himself, "If this man were a prophet, he would have known who and what kind of woman this is who is touching him—that she is a sinner" (39).

The religious authorities get it wrong in many stories, and this is no exception. To the Pharisee, the woman's touch is disgusting; Jesus should be repulsed by her. But I love the fact that the woman no one would ever dream of listening to about matters of faith knows more than the powerful religious man does. She knows that Jesus will not shy away from her touch. She knows that he will see it for what it is: an appeal and a cry from the deepest part of her.

She knows that, for all her past mistakes, she still has the right to touch and be touched by Christ.

Jesus spoke up and said to him, "Simon, I have something to say to you." "Teacher," he replied, "speak." "A certain creditor had two debtors; one owed five hundred denarii, and the other fifty. When they could not pay, he canceled the debts for both of them. Now which of them will love him more?" Simon answered, "I suppose the one for whom he canceled the greater debt." And Jesus said to him, "You have judged rightly." Then turning toward the woman, he said to Simon, "Do you see this woman? I entered your house; you gave me no water for my feet, but she has bathed my feet with her tears and dried them with her hair. You gave me no kiss, but from the time I came in she has not stopped kissing my feet. You did not anoint my head with oil, but she has anointed my feet with ointment. Therefore, I tell you, her sins, which were many, have been forgiven; hence she has shown great love. But the one to whom little is forgiven, loves little" (40–47).

What is the woman thinking as she hears this conversation? Is she afraid to listen, thinking she'll hear Jesus say something that condemns her either directly or indirectly? I suspect not. I believe that by this point, she knows she is safe with Jesus. Jesus has not shrunk away from her touch, nor has he responded to her as other men in the town would, seeing her touch as an invitation to future contact. I like to think that her relief at making contact with someone—contact of an intimate, nonsexual nature—is so great that her healing has already begun, even before Jesus speaks.

Then he said to her, "Your sins are forgiven." But those who were at the table with him began to say among themselves, "Who is this who even forgives sins?" And he said to the woman, "Your faith has saved you; go in peace" (48–50).

It's not specifically mentioned in the Gospel, but I imagine Jesus touching the woman as he says these last few lines. I imagine him bending to her, taking her face carefully in his hands, and looking her right in the eye. Probably it had been a while since anyone had touched her with such honest, gentle affection, no strings attached. I imagine that made the tears start again for her, but this time they were tears of gratitude. And I see her leaving that house in peace—real, beautiful peace.

It touches me deeply, this story, and it does so on many levels. It is a story about the love and forgiveness of Jesus, who sees past our mistakes and recognizes our best, purest selves. It's the story of a God-made-man who doesn't shy away from physical contact with us; instead, he welcomes it and employs its healing power. It is also the story of a woman who bravely trusted her instincts and, even with all her wounds, held on to what she knew to be true. Although everything in her life seemed to argue the opposite, she never lost sight of the fact that touch is, at its core, profoundly good.

Begin

Take a few slow breaths. Center yourself and open up to feel God's presence. Ask for God's grace as you enter this time of prayerful reflection.

Give thanks

Ponder the Incarnation, the fact that God became man and took on a body that could touch and be touched. Give thanks for a God who enters our human experience that way.

Review

When in your life has touch been a healing, positive thing for you?

When has touch been destructive for you? Share this with Jesus. Imagine him comforting you and (if needed) liberating you from your past.

When have you used touch as a way to communicate something too big for words?

Look ahead

Find a few moments in a quiet place. Imagine yourself walking to where Jesus is. Take his hands and tell him what this Gospel story means to you. Imagine him listening to you compassionately and lovingly, showing his love for you through touch. Do this until it feels natural to touch and be touched by Jesus.

Taste

Psalm 34:8 is a curious verse. In the middle of a psalm that is subtitled "Praise for Deliverance from Trouble," we find this directive: "O taste and see that the LORD is good; happy are those who take refuge in him."

At first glance this verse seems oddly out of place. Why taste? Why mention it here, in the context of a poem about how God delivers the righteous?

Perhaps the psalmist used these words because taste is associated with so many positive things that are the opposite of trouble and strife. Taste is associated with food, with nourishment, with the materials that sustain life. It relates to enjoyment, to the pleasures of eating and drinking. It's even associated with romantic love, with the kind of lingering kisses that reflect the emotional bond between two people. Taste and see that the Lord is good; he gives us all these wonderful things.

Most of all, he gives us his incarnate self, Jesus Christ. He comes to us again and again, offering himself as bread and wine. It's divine love that we can taste, and it is the best gift of all.

21

Daily Bread

Where do your meals come from? At any point in your life, and depending on your interpretation of the question, your answer might be one or more of the following:

- From Mom or Dad
- From my spouse
- From farmers far away
- From the vending machine
- From my vegetable garden
- From the supermarket
- From the restaurant on the corner
- From Mexico, Canada, Germany, Thailand, or any other country

The mere fact that there is no one clear answer is proof of something: our daily bread does not come through our own efforts. Even if we are the primary chef in the household, many, many other people are responsible for keeping us nourished and alive.

Cooking is something I really only learned to do once I got married. Prior to that, I subsisted on easy-to-make things (omelets, toasted sandwiches, pasta) and takeout, with the occasional foray into something fancier if people were coming over for dinner. It was hard for me to get excited about learning how to cook for myself alone.

Once I started cooking for Scott as well as myself—and, later, for my two boys—I realized how much effort goes into putting a full meal on the table. It involves making a shopping list, going to the store, putting away food, cooking the food, monitoring pots and pans and temperatures, keeping the cupboard stocked with essentials like olive oil and spices, figuring out which setting on a gas range will cook a pork chop without making it dry and tough. It's a cliché, I know, but I never really understood how much work it was for my mom to make all those meals until I started doing it myself.

It makes up a large part of my daily routine. It takes labor, thought, and planning to feed others.

But lest I start to feel like a meal martyr, I have to realize that I am just one small part of the dinners I serve. Unless you live on a farm with fruit trees and a vegetable garden and are entirely self-sufficient, other people are involved in the food you eat. That bagged lettuce I use as the basis for a salad is possible only because of many other people: the lettuce growers; the pickers; the people who sort, wash, bag; the truckers who transport it to my local supermarket; the market employees who stock the shelves. I can't take all the credit for that salad; I can't even take most of it. To my family, I may be the most visible part of the process, but it's on the table because of the labor, thought, and planning of others.

How easy it is to forget that, and how humbling it is to remember.

Can I thank these people? Some links in the chain are too remote from me, and too anonymous. But there's always some way to acknowledge their efforts. I can care about the working conditions of the migrant pickers I see bent over in the lettuce fields as I drive through California's Central Valley. I can pay attention to legislation that affects them, likewise with laws affecting supermarket workers or restaurant employees. I can make sure my kids know that their meals come not just from me but from countless other people, both near and far away. We can hold those people and their needs in our hearts when we pray each day. And, yes, wherever possible, we can thank the spouse who cooks the meal, the barista who makes the drink, or the waitress who comes to our table balancing our dinners on her forearms.

"Give us this day our daily bread," we pray. Through the hands of others, God does exactly that. And this daily bread is more nourishing when we eat it with gratitude.

Begin

Take a few slow breaths. Center yourself and open up to feel God's presence. Ask for God's grace as you enter this time of prayerful reflection.

Give thanks

Thank God for creation, which provides us with food to satisfy our hunger. Give thanks for all the people who bring food to our plates, from the farmers to the truckers to the cooks to those who serve us at table.

Review

Remember the meals you've enjoyed over the past day. Who made them? Go back through your day and think about the people who made those meals possible, whether they are people you know personally or not. Recognize the goodness of God in their efforts.

For whom have you provided food today? Did you do so graciously, or did you feel resentful about having to serve others?

Think of those in the world, even in your own city, who do not have enough to eat. Are there ways you can help address their need?

Look ahead

Next time you eat something, be mindful of those who are hungry. Think of ways you can help, whether it's praying for them daily or giving of your time or income. If you are cooking for or serving others, let yourself feel the holiness of what you are doing, and serve them with a smile.

22

The No Thank You Bite

Time spent with my six-year-old is never dull. He is always game to try new activities. When he went rock-climbing for the first time at an indoor gym, he nimbly scaled an impossibly high wall while acrophobic Mom cringed below. When he enters a conversation, you never quite know what you're going to get. It could be a multiple-choice question about the solar system; it could be a joke about farting; it could be an astonishingly profound comment about God and heaven. He keeps you guessing.

But when it comes to mealtime, he is as predictable as an episode of *Scooby-Doo*.

At home: "What would you like for lunch, Luke?"

"A cheese sandwich."

At a restaurant: "What would you like to order, Luke?"

"A grilled cheese sandwich."

"What about trying this hamburger? That looks really good."

"No. I want a grilled cheese sandwich."

Maybe it's a good thing that he's comfortable with what he likes. But as a mom, I feel it is my sacred duty to expose him to tastes other than cheddar between two slices of bread (preferably without the crusts). Getting past that gate-keeper—his love of habit, his decision that nothing on earth will taste better than the meal he already knows—is the tough part, particularly when he is reluctant even to taste or try something new.

"I don't like it," is his stock response when someone offers him a food he hasn't tried.

"How do you know? You haven't tried it."

"I don't like it," he says again.

Luckily, at a family dinner at my parents' house, a long-time friend gave me a great tip. It's called the No Thank You Bite, and it goes like this: you can't say "No Thank You" to something unless you have taken at least one bite of it.

In other words, try everything at least once. If you don't, you may never discover your very favorite food.

In my own non-parenting life, I have seen the wisdom of the No Thank You Bite. As a kid, I was convinced I did not like Chinese food. This was based upon a very grave misconception of what Chinese food actually is. Growing up, I associated it with the frozen egg rolls my grandmother and mom would heat up and serve during Super Bowl parties and other occasions that called for snacks. I don't remember the brand name; it was the 1980s, so they probably don't even make them anymore. All I know is that they *looked* exactly like frozen pizza rolls, which I loved, but to bite into those egg rolls was a betrayal. Where you expected cheese and pepperoni, you got cabbage, bits of chicken (I think it was chicken), and other unidentifiable things that put me off of Chinese food for years.

Then, one night when I was in high school, my parents decided we'd go out to dinner.

"Where?" I asked. They named a Chinese restaurant I'd passed a million times and never entered.

"I don't like Chinese food," I said.

"Okay," said my mom. "You don't have to go with us. You can stay home. There are leftovers in the fridge."

Smart mom. I went, and the first bite of that hot and sour soup showed me the error of my ways. I discovered the pleasure of salty, spicy, and sour all mixed together, ladled in a squat ceramic spoon with a groove in the handle like the chute of a waterslide. Throw in some mu-shu pork and lemon chicken, and I was converted.

The No Thank You Bite works. It works even if you're convinced you already know what you like and don't like, and are sure that you can't learn anything new.

Praying is like eating: there are so many flavors out there. When it comes to building a conscious relationship with God—which is how the Jesuit priest William A. Barry defines prayer in his wonderful book *God and You*—there is an entire menu of choices. Over the millennia, countless people have introduced a variety of powerful ways to engage with the divine. Take a look at this list:

- Talking to God about what's on your mind
- Praying the rosary
- Sitting before the Blessed Sacrament in Adoration
- Listing people and situations that are on your mind, then praying on their behalf

- The Examen (both as presented here, and in its other forms)
- Journaling as prayer
- Lectio Divina, which involves reading a Scripture passage several times, letting one word or phrase or verse resonate with you, and reflecting upon it more deeply
- Guided meditation, either with a book or with a prayer leader
- Centering prayer
- Group prayer
- Singing
- Reflecting upon a beautiful piece of music or art
- Walking a labyrinth
- Imagining yourself in a Gospel story
- Praying with the daily Mass readings

I could keep adding to this list. Our prayer life really is like a huge menu or one of those big chalkboards posted above the cash register in a café. There are many new and varied tastes, and when we get stuck in a rut, it's good to break out of our normal routine and order up something different.

One kind of prayer that I've started exploring the past few years is the Ignatian practice of imagining oneself in a Gospel story. To pray this way, you choose a Gospel passage and reread it several times until you know the basic outline by heart. Then you choose someone in the story—it could be a bystander or a key player, such as Peter or the woman at the well or Mary Magdalene—to "be" during the prayer. Close your eyes and enter the story, imagining it unfolding moment by moment with yourself as one of the participants.

This is vastly different from the petitionary prayer I did as a child. In fact, as a kid, I might have thought this sounded too enjoyable to be prayer. (It took me a while to learn that the two are not mutually exclusive.) But every time I've done it, it's been an astonishing way of deepening my relationship with Jesus. He can't remain an abstraction when you are a guest dining with him at the wedding at Cana; he can't feel remote when you are Mary of Bethany, anointing his feet and hearing him chide Judas for criticizing your generosity. Many of my most profound insights about Jesus and about my life in general have come from this particular kind of prayer, one that I tried for the first time in my thirties. It is proof for me that sometimes you need to look at the menu and order something entirely different.

That's not to say that it's bad to do the same kind of prayer over and over if it works for you. It's not the worst thing in the world if my son wants to eat only cheese and wheat bread for lunch and dinner (it's not like he's eating deep-fried

Twinkies). If you have found a kind of prayer that you love, by all means embrace that without guilt. One of my all-time favorite quotations is from the English abbot John Chapman: "Pray as you can," he said, "not as you can't."

At the same time, I've come to realize that expanding our prayer repertoire doesn't contradict this advice; rather, it complements Chapman's wisdom. When you try new things, you discover that there are more ways to pray than you thought—not a bad thing to learn.

So I invite you to turn back the page and take another look at that list. If you see a form of prayer there that intrigues you, resolve to give it a try. And if there's one that you immediately want to reject out of hand, remember the concept of the No Thank You Bite. That new form of prayer just may end up satisfying a hunger you didn't know you had.

Begin

Take a few slow breaths. Center yourself and open up to feel God's presence. Ask for God's grace as you enter this time of prayerful reflection.

Give thanks

Reflect on variety, both in meals and in prayer. Give thanks for the rich tradition of our faith, one that is constantly growing to accommodate new ways of living out our spirituality.

Review

Recall a time when you tried a new food. Where were you—traveling, at a new restaurant, at a friend's house? Did you enjoy it?

When you pray, are you adventurous? Do you feel comfortable trying new forms of prayer?

Think of people you know who have prayer lives or routines that are different from your own. Have you ever spoken to them about why they like that particular prayer practice? Are you willing to try it yourself?

Look ahead

Review the list in this chapter. Pick one of the forms of prayer and commit to trying it at least five times. If you like it, stick with it; if it doesn't work for you, try something else on the list.

23

The Pleasure of Food

A few years ago, something strange happened. For the space of a few days, everything I ate had a bizarre, bitter taste to it.

I simply could not figure it out. Was it some aftereffect of that night-guard fitting at the dentist's office, where they put an awful-tasting goo in my mouth and made me bite down? That seemed unlikely, but no other explanation was forthcoming. If I were a paranoid kind of person, I'd have wondered if someone were trying to poison me (an unfortunate side effect of reading suspense novels), but there was no one in my life who wanted to bump me off (though suspense novels should also have shown me that I wouldn't know it if they did). I simply couldn't explain the chronic bitter taste in my mouth.

Finally, through the wonder of Google, I lit upon an answer. Days earlier, I'd eaten a pasta dish with pine nuts. It turns out that certain inferior-quality pine nuts can, on occasion, have this temporary effect on one's taste buds. Who knew?

Unfortunately, knowing the cause of the bitterness did not make it go away. I had a day or two more in which the pleasure of eating was essentially gone. Nothing tasted the way it was supposed to taste. I ate not for enjoyment but simply to live, and while on the one hand I recognized that this condition would perhaps have the positive advantage of finally getting me back to my pre-motherhood figure, I missed the fun of food. I missed it very much.

When my ability to taste did return, I was delighted. *This is how it's supposed to be*, I thought as I ate my dinner with relish. And believe me, that meal tasted better than ever.

Taste is, perhaps, the sense I take most for granted. As a kid, it was common to have someone pose that perennial question "Would you rather be blind or deaf?" so I'd at least thought about what it would mean to lose each of those senses. I'd known what it was like not to smell when I had a terrible cold. But somehow I had never really thought about losing the ability to taste, because it had never happened before.

We take for granted that food will be enjoyable to eat. We tend to assume that we'll be able to indulge our favorite tastes by going to the supermarket and shopping accordingly, or by going to the restaurant of our choice, or by adding salt or sugar or Sriracha sauce to make something just that much more enjoyable. And yet the more I reflected on this issue, the more I realized that perhaps this ability to taste certain flavors is not actually required for life. As a species, we could, theoretically, get by doing what I did those few tasteless, pine-nut-tainted days: we could eat simply to eat, taking no enjoyment in it.

But what a different world it would be! Without the ability to enjoy different tastes, there would be hardly any cookbooks, no creative chefs or cooking shows. Restaurants as we know them would cease to exist. Grocery stores would shrink without the space needed to stock subtle variations of the same product (cranberry juice with grape? With apple? With raspberry? Whichever one you like!). And though we'd be able to stay alive, our lives would be so very impoverished.

Because there is a tremendous pleasure in eating and drinking things that taste good. You don't realize how pleasurable it is until you can't do it anymore.

This is why there is value to giving up the foods that we love for a while. For Christians, Lent is the traditional time to do this. Everyone knows someone who takes the plunge and makes those forty days a time to give up chocolate, or coffee drinks, or some other taste that is a major part of their daily lives. It is not easy, but it does have an impact, even if you don't entirely stick to the fast.

Case in point: my husband, who loves wine with dinner and the occasional microbrew, once gave up alcohol for Lent. I was mightily impressed at his fortitude. Then, one day in March, I saw him cracking open a beer.

"Hello?" I said pointedly. "Lent?"

"It's St. Patrick's Day," he explained patiently. "That's the feast day of one of the patron saints of our archdiocese. That means you get to suspend your Lenten fast."

"Really," I said. He took a swig and was, clearly, enjoying that beer very much. To his credit, he did not point out the fact that I had not given up a favorite food or drink for Lent and thus had zero credibility in this particular discussion.

But when I have had to give up my favorite tastes—during pregnancy, for example, or other Lents, or for medical reasons—it has been hard, harder than it seems it should be. That fast, that time away from food, has made me realize how often I take for granted the flavors I love. I've learned to appreciate my sacrificed tastes more than ever before. It's not that the food in question tastes better than it used to once I get back to it; it's just that I am more conscious of how much pleasure the sense of taste adds to my life, three times a day and then some.

All this makes me circle back in my mind to the idea of a generous, abundant God. God seems not to want us to eat simply to stay alive. I think of the verse from Isaiah: "On this mountain the LORD of hosts will make for all peoples a feast of rich food, a feast of well-aged wines" (25:6). God promises us deliciousness in the end of time, and we have a taste of it here on earth. Eating is something you have to do to exist, God seems to say, and you might as well enjoy the process. So, he says, I'll make many different kinds of fruits, vegetables, and meats; I'll throw in dairy, nuts, and grains. Now have fun with them. Put them together in creative ways. Try boiling things, roasting them in the sun, marinating, blending. Whatever you do, have fun. I'll enjoy watching you enjoy the foods you create.

But be careful of the pine nuts.

Begin

Take a few slow breaths. Center yourself and open up to feel God's presence. Ask for God's grace as you enter this time of prayerful reflection.

Give thanks

Thank God for the variety of tastes and flavors in the world, for chefs and cooks who find new ways to please our palates.

Review

Think of the past twenty-four hours. What are the best things you tasted?

Think about your life as a whole. What foods or meals stand out to you?

Recall times you went without a certain food due to fasting, pregnancy, illness, or some other reason. What was that like for you? How did it feel to taste that food again?

Look ahead

Try depriving yourself of a favorite food or drink for a time; consider this a mini-Lent. When you do go back to it, savor it more than ever. Make it an opportunity to celebrate the pleasure of that flavor, and to enjoy it as if discovering it for the first time.

24

Kissing

If you want to make a kid utterly and thoroughly disgusted, show that kid a movie in which people share a long, lingering kiss.

Ewwww! They look like they are eating each other! Gross! Brace yourself for one or more of these responses, because you are guaranteed to get them.

Once upon a time I was one of those kids. I was the kid who, if I'd had the power, would have chosen to fast-forward through the entire gazebo scene in *The Sound of Music*. It was boring, boring, boring, except for the kissing parts, which were yucky, yucky, yucky. *I'll never do that*, I said to myself and (probably) out loud.

So much for that resolution.

Fast-forward my own life a few years, and kissing started to sound pretty good to me. Then I did it for the first time, and guess what? It was.

File this under the heading of "Older and Wiser." As you get older, you realize that a kiss—especially when it's done with someone who loves you as much as you love him or her—is one of the best things you can do with your mouth.

So maybe it's not a surprise that kissing is so often spoken of in relation to those other very pleasurable mouth-y pastimes: eating and drinking. And this connection is hardly modern; it's biblical.

In the short book of the Song of Solomon in the Old Testament, a groom and his bride speak of their delight in each other's physical presence. Fittingly, the book is a hymn to the senses. There are many descriptions of the physical beauty of each lover; fragrance is often invoked as well. And, most notably to me when I reread it, there are many references to taste.

The book starts off with the bride speaking of her groom: "Let him kiss me with the kisses of his mouth! For your love is better than wine" (1:2). In the next chapter, she rhapsodizes: "His fruit was sweet to my taste" (2:3). The groom, not to be outdone, is just as enthusiastic about the sensory delights of his beloved: "How much better is your love than wine" (4:10). The next verse continues the theme: "Your lips distill nectar, my bride; honey and milk are under your tongue" (4:11). Later, the groom speaks to his beloved, saying, "O may your breasts be like clusters of the vine, and the scent of your breath like apples, and your kisses like the best wine that goes down smoothly, gliding over lips and teeth" (7:8–9).

If I were a kid, I'd have been pressing the fast-forward button by the second verse.

But since I'm no longer a kid, I love what this chapter is saying. I love that it is a totally frank celebration of the beauty of physical intimacy. I love that it is a paean to kissing: the bride and groom are utterly unabashed about how intoxicating it is to put lips to lips, like sipping the best wine. There's no shame in doing so. It makes you want more and more and more. And I love that all this is found in the Bible.

Over the centuries, scholars (and many regular folk) have interpreted the Song of Solomon as a metaphor for God's love for his people. God loves us with the same intensity and fire and passion that the bride and groom have for each other. God wants to love us so completely that our toes curl, that we lose ourselves in that love only to find ourselves.

It is probably safe to say that not all of us were raised with this image of God. In fact, many Catholics have had the opposite experience, taught implicitly or explicitly that there needs to be a polite distance between God and us (and between ourselves and one another). And yet, throughout the history of the Catholic Church, certain people have instinctively understood the image of God as a lover. St. Teresa of Ávila is one; her writings describe the heavenly visions she received, visions that left her in physical ecstasy. The famous statue sculpted by Bernini depicts her during one of these visions, her head tilted back with an expression that can best be described as the look of someone at the moment of sexual climax. It's kind of shocking the first time you see it.

But when you think about the metaphor of God as lover, it works. When you are kissing a lover, you can't get much closer. You are tasting that person, which is something we almost never do in any other context but romantic love. There is an intimacy that can't be denied; there is no distance between you. You are so on fire with desire for this person that normal, conventional ways of expressing affection are not sufficient. Is it such a stretch to imagine God doing that for us? And is it such a stretch to see our physical relationships as an echo of this divine abandon? Maybe if the Catholic Church has made a big deal out of sex for all these centuries, it's because it is powerful and good and because we can enjoy it most when we take it seriously.

And when a physical relationship is right, the Song of Solomon says, don't take it for granted. Enjoy it to the maximum. Be like the bride and groom, two young warm-blooded lovers, playful and passionate and eager. Touch and kiss and savor the taste of each other, a taste that is sweeter than honey and more exhilarating than wine.

Begin

Take a few slow breaths. Center yourself and open up to feel God's presence. Ask for God's grace as you enter this time of prayerful reflection.

Give thanks

Reflect on physical intimacy. Give gratitude for a God who gives us many ways to understand his love for us, including the metaphor of lovers.

Review

If you are currently in a physical relationship with someone, think about the evolution of that relationship. What was it like to kiss that person for the first time? Remember that moment, and the feeling of excitement and discovery.

Has the physical side of your relationship grown dull? If so, think about why, and about how you can rekindle it. (Some long, leisurely kissing may be just the thing.)

Do you desire intimacy but don't have it at this point in your life? What do the passages about the lovers bring up for you—longing, wistfulness, hope, envy? Bring that to God in prayer.

Think of God being as eager to be with you as the bride and groom are to be with each other. Is that a comfortable image for you? Why or why not?

Look ahead

Read a portion (or all) of the Song of Solomon. Go slowly, letting yourself fully ponder each image. Keep reminding yourself that what you are reading is Scripture, and cast aside all images of a killjoy God. Let the image of a passionate God slowly sink into your soul.

25

The Eucharist

Second grade, St. Simon School. It was spring, and we were preparing for our first Holy Communion. My teacher was Sister Agnes, a woman in her seventies who stood about five feet tall. She was from Philadelphia and, like all of our sisters, wore a navy-blue habit and dark veil. She pronounced "beautiful" by drawing out every syllable: "bee-you-tea-full."

I am sure that particular adjective got frequent use during our preparations to receive the Eucharist for the first time. Sister was quite reverent in her explanation of the huge rite of passage that was about to occur, and my blue-plaid companions and I were well-trained. We went through many dress rehearsals, walking in a straight, single-file line to the front of the room where Sister, playing the priest, held up an imaginary host and said, "The body of Christ" before pretending to put it into our cupped hands.

"Amen," we responded, one by one, lifting the host with our right hands and miming putting it in our mouths. We then made a well-executed ninety-degree turn to the left and reverently filed back to our seats. In the church, of course, we would not sit but would kneel down, hands clasped, and pray silently.

The movements were clear. The posture was clear. The script was clear. But there was one huge unanswered question: what did Jesus taste like?

It's a perfectly natural question coming from a group of eight-year-olds, and speculation was rife. One of my classmates shared the rumor that the host tasted like Styrofoam. Sister Agnes could not positively deny that—after all, who *has* tasted Styrofoam?—but as I recall, she didn't spend a great deal of time on the matter of taste. Maybe this was due to the fact that her own First Communion was more than sixty years in the past at that point, and her memories of her own curiosity had faded. I also suspect that when it came to the Eucharist, she didn't find the issue of taste to be the most important question.

Now, having consumed numerous hosts over my forty-odd years of life, I am inclined to agree with Sister Agnes.

What Jesus tastes like is not the most pressing question. Here's one that is far more compelling: why would Jesus take the appearance of bread and wine and let himself be eaten?

Because, honestly, the entire concept is very, very strange.

It was not until my twenties that the strangeness of it all really hit home. I happened to be in the church at Stanford, overhearing a training session for Eucharistic ministers. The liturgist was giving some background on the scriptural basis for the real presence and also on its history.

"When the first Christians were gathering for the Lord's Supper, consuming the bread and wine that they said was the body and blood of Christ," she said, "outsiders struggled with that. To them, it sounded like cannibalism."

What? I had to stop and think. The ritual I'd been doing for years, automatically, without thinking—cannibalism? I started to think about how I would explain this part of the Mass to someone who was not Catholic. What would I say? "Well, the priest says the words of the Last Supper over the bread and wine, and then they become the body and blood of Jesus, and then, um, we eat them." Had I not been a cradle Catholic, raised to see this mysterious sacrament as something normal, I'd find it shocking too. As a cradle Catholic thinking about it objectively for the first time ever, I realized that it *was* shocking.

It was not so shocking that I stopped taking Communion, but it was no longer something I could do casually. I still filed down the aisle, tasted the dry crackle on my tongue, and sipped the sweet wine, but I was aware, in a way I had not been before, that I was consuming Christ. The body of Christ was entering my body. That fact was astonishing.

And it led me to that all-important question: why? Why would Jesus, at the Last Supper, leave us this legacy of himself as food and drink? I won't try to address the historical and theological reasons why; I'll leave that to the scholars. But I will say that, over the years, as my understanding of Mass has become more layered and nuanced thanks to the growing experiences of my life outside of church, I've come to realize a few things about this sacrament, things that have satisfied my curiosity and may perhaps satisfy yours.

One thing I have pondered is the implication of God becoming something we can taste. It's probably safe to say that of the five senses, the sense of taste is the one least used in our interactions with other people. There's almost a hierarchy of use with the five senses. Over the course of our lives, we see lots of people; we hear almost as many as we see. When we are a certain distance from people, we are able to smell them; come a little closer, and we can touch them.

But how many people do we actually taste? Nursing infants taste their mothers; lovers taste each other; that's about it. It's a very tiny circle of people.

It strikes me that these two relationships happen to have something in common: intimacy. I would suspect that if you did a survey and asked people who in their lives knows them better than anyone else, mothers and lovers would be the most popular answers. Mothers remember what we were like when we were too young to know ourselves; lovers experience us in ways that all other people do not.

And through the Eucharist, we taste Jesus, too. That tiny circle grows larger. He fits beautifully into this company, this small community of people who happen to be privy to our truest selves. In fact, he's closer to us than the others because he has known us from the very start, even before our mothers did. Likewise, he sees all sides of us, even the parts we choose to hide from our nearest and dearest.

It's quite intimate, letting yourself be tasted, and I love that Jesus goes there. I love the implications of this, how he pulls out all the stops to connect with us in the most profound way possible. If you aren't finding me through any of the other four ways I'm trying to reach you, he says, I'll try this most intimate one. I gave you five senses, and I will make myself available through every single one of them—even if it means that the Savior of the world takes the form of a speck of bread held in an eight-year-old's cupped hands.

One challenging aspect of the Eucharist is how visceral and direct it is. This becomes pretty unmistakable when you read the Gospel passages relating to the sacrament. In the Gospel of John, Jesus tells his followers, "Very truly, I tell you, unless you eat the flesh of the Son of Man and drink his blood, you have no life in you" (John 6:53). Understandably, he lost a few disciples over this bizarre statement, especially when they challenged him on it and he doubled down. How would I have reacted, hearing that? Probably not well. The idea of eating flesh and drinking blood would have sounded macabre, so beyond the pale. Why on earth would I do that? Why on earth would this man think that I would?

But as I sat in class on that long-ago day in college with these feelings and let them simmer below the surface of my newly energized Catholic faith, a memory surfaced out of the deepest recesses of my mind. It was a news story I'd heard years earlier about an earthquake in some faraway part of the world. It was the story of a mother and her child who had been trapped in the rubble for days before being rescued. They had no food and no water. And with nothing else to do, the mother cut herself and fed her child drops of her own blood, which kept the child alive until they were rescued.

I'm a wimp, so I remember wincing when I first heard that story. But following the wince was what can only be described as a tremor of awe. Every now and then you catch a glimpse of life stripped to its barest meaning and humanity at its absolute finest. The mother gave her own physical body to keep her child alive. She offered herself as food, feeding her child, as moms always do, and yet feeding her with her own blood, making herself seemingly less so that someone else could have life. And the net effect was that both were saved.

It occurred to me that this story was the story of the Eucharist, in a different setting. Jesus loves us as this mother loved her child, desperately and fiercely, with a gesture so astonishing that you can't ignore it. He gives his very self to nourish us, not in some abstract and airy way but in a way that is elemental—flesh and blood. We didn't ask for it; maybe we do not even know how much we need it. But every Mass it is offered again. The taste of the host on our tongue is a promise that no matter what else may seem to lie smashed and broken around us, Life goes on giving us life.

It's an astonishing thing, the Eucharist. I watched my older son make his first Holy Communion, and although his teacher prepared him well, I recognize that it's one of those mysteries that we simply need to grow into. It takes time and life experience to digest it all. And in spite of all of my adult awareness, sometimes I still find myself slipping into complacency as I go up the center aisle at Mass. In fact, there is nothing mundane about the sacrament. This ritual is the very heart of my faith, and it tells me everything I need to know about Jesus. He gave himself for me; he wants to be as close to me as possible. He will do whatever it takes to keep me alive.

So what does the body of Jesus taste like? Thirty-four years after my first communion, I think I finally have a good answer. It tastes like intimacy and sacrifice and love—and the greatest of these is love.

Begin

Take a few slow breaths. Center yourself and open up to feel God's presence. Ask for God's grace as you enter this time of prayerful reflection.

Give thanks

Express your gratitude for the God who became man and who offers himself as bread and wine for us. Give thanks for a faith that allows you to have this direct encounter with Jesus, every day if you wish.

Review

Remember your first experience of communion. What was it like for you? Do you recall how you felt about tasting the body of Jesus for the first time?

Think about other experiences of communion. Can you identify any that were particularly powerful, when the meaning of the sacrament made itself clear to you?

Recall the story of the mother and child. For whom would you make such a sacrifice? Think of Christ offering that love to everyone without reservation.

Look ahead

The next time you receive communion, think about a God who offers himself as something we can eat. Let yourself feel the intimacy of what Christ is giving us, and savor the taste of his astonishing love.

Epilogue

It was a Sunday morning at St. Dominic's in San Francisco. Sunlight shone through the high stained-glass windows and illuminated the gray stonework. Mass was in full swing, and I sat with my younger son, who was nine months old, on my lap.

As I sat there in the pew, periodically getting up to walk him down the side aisles when he grew restless, I wondered how he was experiencing the Mass. Too young to understand the homily or to grasp what was happening up there on the altar, what was he absorbing? What kind of impressions would leave their imprint on his memory, like a baby hand in clay?

I realized that there were the things he could see: the gray stone walls, the sunlight, the bright primary colors of the stained glass, the glow of the candles.

Also, the things he could hear: the voices of the priest and lectors, the music of the choir, the communal responses of hundreds of worshippers saying words that people have said for centuries.

There were the things he could smell: leftover incense, the lingering scent of candle smoke, the smell of wood varnish on the pews.

And also the things he could touch: the smooth curved backs of the pews, the wooden carvings decorating the confessionals as I paused in the side aisle and let him run his hands over the doors.

And later, in about eight years' time, there would be the things he could taste: the body and blood of Christ in the form of bread and wine, the most powerful example of God's goodness and the reason for our presence there on that Sunday morning.

As I pondered all this, I realized once again that this is why my Catholic faith makes sense. It makes sense because it engages the senses. It reflects the reality we find in our lives outside of church: God speaks to us not only through our hearts but also through our eyes, ears, nose, fingers, lips.

That morning in my arms, my baby was learning this reality. He was learning it without even knowing he was doing so. And yet my own journey has shown that life is so much richer when we do know it, when an awareness of the spirituality of the senses finds its way into our minds and prayers and conversations.

For all of life's mysteries, this much I know for sure: we live in a world of good. We live in a world where God fills every one of our senses, loving us enough to meet us exactly where we are.

Suggestions for Further Prayer

If you'd like to continue exploring the spirituality of the senses, here are some prayer practices to try:

1) Every evening, pray a mini-Examen focusing on the five senses.

- Where did I see God?
- Where did I hear God's voice?
- What did I smell that made me think of God?
- How did God speak to me through touch today?
- What did I taste that helped me understand God's goodness?

It might be helpful to take notes as you pray, jotting down your answers to the questions above. This may help you notice not only God's patterns but also God's surprises, and could be rewarding to read again during spiritual dry spells.

2) Challenge yourself to put a sensory experience into words. Describe (either verbally or in writing) a sunset, a comfortable shirt, or a favorite meal as carefully as you can, as if for someone who has not experienced it. This kind of exercise is helpful because it trains us to pay closer attention to our sensory experiences and to be more conscious of them as they are happening.

3) The Bible is full of stories and passages that relate to the senses. Take some time to read and reflect on these passages. Think of what each one reveals about the sense involved.

- Sight: the Transfiguration (Matthew 17:1–8)
- Touch: Jesus and the woman with the hemorrhage (Luke 8:43–48)
- Taste: the wedding at Cana (John 2:1–11)
- Hearing: Elijah and the still small voice (1 Kings 19:11–13)
- Smell: Mary of Bethany anoints Jesus (John 12:1–8)

4) Memorize some Bible passages relating to the senses. Here are some good ones:

- Taste and see that the LORD is good. (Psalm 34:8)

- The people who walked in darkness have seen a great light. (Isaiah 9:2)
- Let anyone with ears to hear listen. (Mark 4:9)

Keep these passages in the pocket of your memory. Repeat them to yourself throughout the day: when you wake up, on your way to work, at quiet moments on the job or at home, before turning in at night. Let the sounds of these words become as natural as breathing.

5) St. Ignatius was a big fan of engaging the senses in prayer. One prayer method he advocated was to imagine yourself as one of the people in a Gospel story. Here's how:

a. Choose a Gospel passage that speaks to you. It's best to choose one that involves action of some kind.

b. Reread the passage until you know it by heart. Decide which character in the story you will be—a bystander, an apostle, one of the people who interacts directly with Jesus.

c. Close the Bible. Find a comfortable place to sit. Close your eyes and imagine the setting. What do you see, hear, smell? If touch or taste figures in the story, imagine those details as well. Don't worry about making your setting perfectly faithful to the period; this is more about making an *emotional* connection to the story than about historical accuracy. Let the impressions and images come to you without judging them or trying to make the scenario perfect.

d. Let the Gospel story unfold, imagining yourself as part of it. What do you think or feel as you hear, see, and perhaps touch Jesus? What enters your mind as you see others interact with him? Pay attention to your emotions. Be open to surprises and to what God wants to reveal to you through this exercise.

e. After concluding this prayer, take a few moments to reflect upon the insights you gained. Many people (myself included) find that this exercise not only helps them understand Jesus as a real, living person, but it also helps them gain insight into the most pressing issues they are facing.

Some stories that are particularly good for engaging the senses:

- Jesus and the death of Lazarus (John 11:17–44)
- The healing of the paralytic (Mark 2:1–12)
- The baptism of Jesus (Matthew 3:13–17)
- Jesus' response to the woman caught in adultery (John 8:1–11)
- The wedding at Cana (John 2:1–11)

- The storm at sea (Mark 4:35–41)
- The road to Emmaus (Luke 24:13–35)
- Jesus cooking the fish at the Sea of Galilee (John 21:1–14)

Acknowledgments

Every writer should have someone like Joe Durepos (or, even better, Joe Durepos himself) to help her navigate her way from idea to manuscript. I'm similarly blessed to work with editor *extraordinaire* Vinita Hampton Wright. I also want to give a shout-out to Tom McGrath, Fr. Paul Campbell, Andrew Yankech, Rosemary Lane, Denise Gorss, Ray Ives, the fabulous Becca Russo, and all the other folk at Loyola Press. It's a joy to know such talented (and, frankly, just plain fun) people.

I'm grateful for the support of friends and colleagues, especially Tarn Wilson. Thanks also to my parents and sister, Amy, for their encouragement and to Matthew and Luke for letting Mommy escape to Peet's with her laptop every now and then to finish a chapter.

The biggest thanks go to Scott, who answers theological questions, encourages my gifts, and helps me juggle all the various pieces of my life. I'm one lucky woman.

Finally, my gratitude to the sisters and priests and teachers of my childhood, who built a foundation that was more solid than I knew.

About the Author

Ginny Kubitz Moyer is the author of *Random MOMents of Grace: Experiencing God in the Adventures of Motherhood* and *Mary and Me: Catholic Women Reflect on the Mother of God* (winner of a Catholic Press Award). Her writing has appeared in many print and online publications, including U.S. Catholic and St. Anthony Messenger. She lives with her family in the San Francisco Bay Area and blogs at RandomActsofMomness.com.

Also Available

 **An Ignatian Book of Days**
$12.95 | 4145-1 | PB

 **A Simple, Life-Changing Prayer**
$9.95 | 3535-1 | PB

 **God Finds Us**
$9.95 | 3827-7 | PB

 **Reimagining the Ignatian Examen**
$9.95 | 4244-1 | PB

TO ORDER, call 800.621.1008, visit www.loyolapress.com
or visit your local bookseller.

Also Available

Daily Inspiration for Women
Seasons of a Woman's Life

Ginny Kubitz Moyer, Jessica Mesman Griffith, Margaret Silf, Vinita Hampton Wright

$12.95 • Paperback • 4041-6

A Catholic Woman's Book of Days

Amy Welborn

$12.95 • Paperback • 2057-9

Random MOMents of Grace
Experiencing God in the Adventures of Motherhood

Ginny Kubitz Moyer

$13.95 • Paperback • 3840-6

Ignatian Spirituality Online
www.ignatianspirituality.com

Visit us online to

- Join our *E-Magis* newsletter

- Pray the Daily Examen

- Make an online retreat with the *Ignatian Prayer Adventure*

- Participate in the conversation with the dotMagis blog and at **facebook.com/ignatianspirituality**

3-Minute Retreat

3 minutes a day can give you 24 hours of peace.

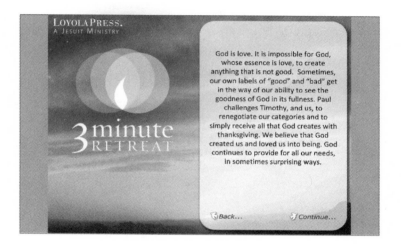

The *3-Minute Retreat* invites you to take a short prayer break at your computer. Spend some quiet time reflecting on a Scripture passage and preparing your heart and mind for the day ahead.

Sign up to receive a daily invitation to reflect, delivered to your inbox every morning.

Join the conversation at
facebook.com/3MinuteRetreat